Implementing the Tax Transparency Standards

A HANDBOOK FOR ASSESSORS AND JURISDICTIONS

Second Edition

OECD

This work is published on the responsibility of the Secretary-General of the OECD. The opinions expressed and arguments employed herein do not necessarily reflect the official views of the Organisation or of the governments of its member countries.

Please cite this publication as:
OECD (2011), *Implementing the Tax Transparency Standards: A Handbook for Assessors and Jurisdictions, Second Edition*, OECD Publishing.
http://dx.doi.org/10.1787/9789264110496-en

ISBN 978-92-64-10723-6 (print)
ISBN 978-92-64-11049-6 (PDF)

Corrigenda to OECD publications may be found on line at: *www.oecd.org/publishing/corrigenda*.

Table of contents

INTRODUCTION **5**

About the Global Forum **7**

About this Handbook **9**

The Peer Review Process **13**

PART I: KEY DOCUMENTS OF THE GLOBAL FORUM FOR PEER REVIEWS **17**

Terms of Reference **21**

I. Introduction 21
II. The Standards of Transparency and Exchange of Information for Tax Purposes 22
III. Output of the Peer Review Process 32
Annex 1 – Peer Review Group Mandate 35
Annex 2 – Sources of the Internationally Agreed Standards on Transparency and Effective Exchange of Information for Tax Purposes (the Standards) 37

Revised Methodology for Peer Review and Non-Member Reviews **43**

I. Introduction 43
II. Peer Reviews 45
III. Procedures for Reports on Non-Members 60
IV. Funding 61
Annex 3 – Summary of the Key Responsibilities of Participants in a Review 63
Annex 4 –Model Assessment Schedules 69
Annex 5 – Chart on the Procedure to Adopt Reports 71
Annex 6 – Outline of Peer Review Report 73

Assessment Criteria **75**

Introduction 75
The Goal of the Rating System 75
The Structure of the Rating System 77
Application of the Rating System 80
Conclusion 82

PART II: MAIN SOURCES OF STANDARDS 83

Article 26 of the OECD Model Tax Convention on Income and on Capital and its Commentary 85

The 2002 Model Agreement on Exchange of Information on Tax Matters and its Commentary 103

Enabling Effective Exchange of Information: Availability and Reliability Standard The Joint Ad Hoc Group on Accounts (JAHGA) Report 149

The 2006 OECD Manual on Information Exchange – Module on General and Legal Aspects of Exchange of Information 163

The 2006 OECD Manual on Information Exchange – Module 1 on Exchange of Information on Request 193

The OECD's Project on Harmful Tax Practices Consolidated Application Note Guidance in Applying the 1998 Report to Preferential Tax Regimes 209

INTRODUCTION

About the Global Forum

The Global Forum on Transparency and Exchange of Information for Tax Purposes is the multilateral framework within which work in the area of tax transparency and exchange of information is carried out by over 100 jurisdictions which participate in the work of the Global Forum on an equal footing.

The Global Forum is charged with in-depth monitoring and peer review of the implementation of the standards of transparency and exchange of information for tax purposes. These standards are primarily reflected in the 2002 OECD Model Agreement on Exchange of Information on Tax Matters and its commentary, and in Article 26 of the OECD Model Tax Convention on Income and on Capital and its commentary as updated in 2004, which has been incorporated in the UN Model Tax Convention.

The standards provide for international exchange on request of foreseeably relevant information for the administration or enforcement of the domestic tax laws of a requesting party. Fishing expeditions are not authorised but all foreseeably relevant information must be provided, including bank information and information held by fiduciaries, regardless of the existence of a domestic tax interest or the application of a dual criminality standard.

All members of the Global Forum, as well as jurisdictions identified by the Global Forum as relevant to its work, are being reviewed. This process is undertaken in two phases. Phase 1 reviews assess the quality of a jurisdiction's legal and regulatory framework for the exchange of information, while Phase 2 reviews look at the practical implementation of that framework. Some Global Forum members are undergoing combined – Phase 1 plus Phase 2 – reviews. The ultimate goal is to help jurisdictions to effectively implement the international standards of transparency and exchange of information for tax purposes.

All review reports are published once adopted by the Global Forum and they thus represent agreed Global Forum reports.

For more information on the work of the Global Forum on Transparency and Exchange of Information for Tax Purposes, and for copies of the published review reports, please refer to www.oecd.org/tax/transparency.

About this Handbook

This handbook is intended to assist the assessment teams and the reviewed jurisdictions that are participating in the Global Forum on Transparency and Exchange of Information (the Global Forum) peer reviews and non-member reviews. It provides contextual background information on the Global Forum and the peer review process. It also contains relevant key documents and authoritative sources that will guide assessors and reviewed jurisdictions throughout the peer review process. Assessors should be familiar with the information and documents contained in this handbook as it will assist in conducting proper and fair assessments. This handbook is also a unique source of information for governments, academics and others interested in transparency and exchange of information for tax purposes.

Background

Tax avoidance and tax evasion threaten government revenues throughout the world. Globalisation generates opportunities to increase global wealth but also results in increased risks. With the increase in cross-border flows of capital that come with a global financial system, tax administrations around the world face more and greater challenges to the proper enforcement of their tax laws than ever before. To meet these challenges, tax authorities must increasingly rely on international co-operation based on the implementation of international standards of transparency and effective exchange of information. Better transparency and information exchange for tax purposes are key to ensuring that corporate and individual taxpayers have no safe haven to hide their income and assets and that they pay the right amount of tax in the right place.

The Organisation for Economic Co-operation and Development ("OECD") has been the leading organisation in promoting high standards of transparency and exchange of information for tax purposes and initiated by the OECD, the Global Forum has been the driving force behind the development and acceptance of the international standards of tax transparency and exchange of information. The Global Forum was created in 2000 to provide an inclusive forum for achieving high standards of transparency and exchange of information in a way that is equitable and permits fair competition between all jurisdictions, large and small, OECD and non-OECD.

The standards of transparency and effective exchange of information for tax purposes are primarily reflected in the 2002 OECD's Model Agreement on Exchange of Information on Tax Matters (the OECD Model TIEA) and its commentary and in Article 26 of the OECD Model Tax Convention on Income and on Capital (the OECD Model Tax Convention) and its commentary as updated in 2004 (and approved by the OECD Council on 15 July 2005). The revisions to Article 26 aimed at reflecting the work that the Global Forum has done have also been incorporated in the United Nations Model Double Taxation Convention between Developed and Developing Countries (the UN Model Tax Convention).[1] The texts of both the Model TIEA and Article 26 of the Model Tax Convention are contained in this handbook.

The standards provide for exchange on request of foreseeably relevant information for the administration or enforcement of the domestic tax laws of a requesting party. Fishing expeditions are not authorised but all foreseeably relevant information must be provided, including bank information and information held by fiduciaries, regardless of the existence of a domestic tax interest or the application of a dual criminality standard.

From 2006, the Global Forum has published annual assessments of the legal and administrative framework for transparency and exchange of information in over 80 countries. The latest annual assessment can be accessed on the Global Forum public website: *www.oecd.org/tax/transparency.*

The Global Forum's Mandate

International tax evasion is now high on the agenda of political leaders, reflecting tax scandals that have affected a number of countries around the world and the spotlight that the global financial crisis has put on international tax evasion generally. The need to tackle cross-border tax evasion is not new, but it has been lent a new urgency by the emphasis which has been put on it by G20 leaders, the OECD and other international organisations. There is now a widespread recognition that all jurisdictions need to implement the international standards of transparency and exchange of information for tax purposes if international tax evasion is to be tackled effectively.

[1] Article 26 of the UN Model Tax Convention is similar to Article 26 of the OECD Model Tax Convention subject to paragraph 1, which inserts the phrase "and in particular for the prevention of fraud or evasion of such taxes" in the first sentence, the phrase "and where originally regarded as secret in the transmitting State" in the fourth sentence and adds a new 6th sentence.

Political attention to the Global Forum's work, and the urgency of ensuring that high standards of transparency and exchange of information are in place around the world, made it imperative to review the Global Forum's structure and mandate. To do this, the Global Forum met in Mexico in September 2009 to discuss progress made in implementing the international standards of transparency and exchange of information, and how to respond to international calls to strengthen the work of the Global Forum. Participants agreed that the Global Forum will:

- carry out an in-depth monitoring and peer review of the implementation of the standards of transparency and exchange of information for tax purposes;
- develop multilateral instruments to speed up negotiations; and
- ensure that developing countries benefit from the new environment of transparency.

In addition, the Global Forum now has a 15-member Steering Group and a 30-member Peer Review Group. The first meetings of the Peer Review Group took place in October and December 2009 and delegates have worked diligently to lay the foundations for the peer reviews, which began in March 2010.

Purpose of the Peer Reviews

The Global Forum is undertaking a robust, transparent and accelerated process of reviews of the implementation of the international standards of transparency and exchange of information for tax purposes. Assessment teams, comprising representatives from Global Forum member jurisdictions, along with members of the Global Forum Secretariat, are conducting systematic examinations and assessments of jurisdictions' legal and regulatory frameworks for transparency and exchange of information for tax purposes and also of the jurisdictions' practical application of their frameworks. The ultimate goal is to help jurisdictions to effectively implement the international standards of transparency and exchange of information for tax purposes.

The effectiveness of the Global Forum reviews relies, in part, on the influence and open dialogue between jurisdictions during the peer review process and also on the public nature of the outcomes of this process. The peer review process involves a mix of formal recommendations in the peer review reports and informal dialogue by the peer jurisdictions, public scrutiny, and the impact on all of the above on domestic public opinion, national administrations and policy makers. This aids understanding of various ways in which the standards can be implemented in domestic systems and stimulates jurisdictions to strengthen their legal and regulatory frameworks, and the effectiveness of their frameworks, in order to meet the international standards of transparency and exchange of information for tax purposes.

The Peer Review Process

In General

All members of the Global Forum, as well as jurisdictions identified by the Global Forum as relevant to its work, are undergoing reviews of their implementation of the standards of transparency and exchange of information in tax matters. The reviews take place in two phases. Phase 1 reviews examine the legal and regulatory framework for transparency and the exchange of information for tax purposes. Phase 2 reviews look into the implementation of the standards in practice. Combined reviews evaluate both the legal and regulatory framework (Phase 1) and the implementation of the standards in practice (Phase 2).

The core output of the peer review process comes in the form of a final report. The reports identify and describe the strengths and any shortcomings that exist and provide recommendations as to how the shortcomings might by addressed by the reviewed jurisdiction.

Peer review reports reflect information and input from a variety of sources, including input provided by peer jurisdictions, information and data provided by the reviewed jurisdiction, and independent research conducted by assessment teams. In both Phase 1 and Phase 2 reviews, input from peer jurisdictions is solicited at the beginning of the review process. This is accomplished by way of a general call for comments for Phase 1 reviews and by way of a questionnaire for Phase 2 reviews. Depending on the type of review, a Phase 1 or a Phase 2 questionnaire is used to solicit information from the reviewed jurisdiction. The reviewed jurisdiction is also to make documents and data available to the assessment team. The questionnaires used in the peer review process allow the assessment team to have a clear roadmap to conduct the review, which in turn will ensure that the review is consistent with other reviews and is complete.

There are three core documents elaborated by the Global Forum for conducting the reviews: the Terms of Reference, which breaks down the standards into their essential elements and enumerated aspects; the Methodology for Peer Reviews and Non-Member Reviews, which provides detailed guidance on the procedural aspects of the reviews; and the Assessment Criteria, which establishes a system for assessing the implementation of the standards.

Role of the Assessors

The reviews are managed by an assessment team, usually consisting of two expert assessors and a member from the Secretariat.

The members of the assessment team represent the Global Forum in carrying out the review. Assessors do not act in their official capacity as representatives of their respective jurisdictions. The assessment team undertakes this role in an objective and fair manner, free from any influence of national interest that could undermine the credibility of the peer review process.

The role of the assessment team is to ensure the peer review is impartial, transparent, comprehensive and multilateral. The peer review is conducted on a non-adversarial basis, and relies heavily on mutual trust among the assessment team and reviewed jurisdiction, as well as shared confidence in the process.

Assessors should be aware of the workload that is involved in participating in the peer review process and must take this into account relative to their own national commitments. The peer review process requires a significant commitment, before, during and after the review, leading to the adoption of the final report. By agreeing to participate in this process, assessors undertake to work as a team in a collaborative and timely fashion.

Role of the Assessed Jurisdiction

Participation in the peer review by the reviewed jurisdiction implies the duty to co-operate with the assessment team, the Peer Review Group and the Secretariat by, amongst other things: making documents and data available; responding to questions and requests for information; and facilitating contacts and hosting on-site visits. For a review of non-members of the Global Forum, co-operation and involvement of the reviewed jurisdiction is invited, but if necessary the review will proceed in any event using the best available information. The individuals responsible for participating on behalf of the reviewed jurisdiction could include representatives from the jurisdiction's competent authority as well as other civil servants from relevant Ministries and government agencies.

Role of the Secretariat

The Secretariat provides an interface between the work of the assessors and that of the reviewed jurisdiction, co-ordinating schedules and processes of the review. The Secretariat works with the assessors to review all relevant information and provide supplementary questions to the jurisdiction being reviewed. The Secretariat plays an important role in co-ordinating preparation of the first draft of the report, and integrating the input of assessors and the reviewed jurisdiction. Finally, the Secretariat is responsible for facilitating the consideration and approval of the report by the Peer Review Group and its adoption by the Global Forum.

Confidentiality

Respect for principles of confidentiality ensures each participant in the peer review process the freedom to engage in open, honest review. Material produced by members of the Global Forum concerning an assessed jurisdiction (*e.g.* responses to the questionnaire, proposed questions for the assessed jurisdiction and responses by the assessed jurisdiction) are treated as confidential and are not made publicly available. Additionally, material produced by an assessed jurisdiction during a review (*e.g.* documents describing a jurisdiction's regime, responses to the questionnaire, or responses to assessors' queries) and by the Secretariat or assessors (*e.g.* reports from assessors, draft reports) are treated as confidential and are not made publicly available, unless the assessed jurisdiction and the Secretariat consent to their release. Assessors should not retain copies of submitted material and should not use the content of any submitted material for any purpose unrelated to the peer review process.

PART I: KEY DOCUMENTS OF THE GLOBAL FORUM FOR PEER REVIEWS

Key Documents of the Global Forum for Peer Reviews

This section briefly describes the core documents elaborated by the Global Forum for conducting the reviews, authoritative sources setting out the standards on transparency and effective exchange of information for tax purposes, and additional sources that may be useful to assessors, the Peer Review Group and the Global Forum in applying the standards in the peer review process. Copies of these documents can be found following this overview.

Core Documents for the Reviews

Terms of Reference

The Terms of Reference describes the standards on transparency and exchange of information for tax purposes and breaks them down into 10 essential elements to be assessed through the review process. The essential elements themselves are further broken down into 31 enumerated aspects. The Terms of Reference are used by assessment teams as the key elements against which jurisdictions' legal and regulatory framework and actual implementation of the standards are assessed. It also serves as the basis for the Phase 1 and Phase 2 questionnaires. The Terms of Reference are based on primary authoritative sources (see B) and complimentary authoritative sources (See C).

Revised Methodology for Peer Reviews and Non-Member Reviews

The revised Methodology for Peer Reviews and Non-Member Reviews sets forth detailed procedures and guidelines for the peer reviews of members of the Global Forum and the equivalent reviews of non-members. It provides:

- details on the creation of assessment teams;
- procedures for obtaining input from partner jurisdictions and receiving responses from the assessed jurisdiction;
- guidance on the on-site visits;
- the key responsibilities of each of the participants in the peer review process;
- model assessment schedules;

- the procedures for adoption of a report;
- the procedures for following-up reports; and
- an outline of the peer review reports.

Assessment Criteria

The Assessment Criteria establishes a system for assessing the implementation of the standards in Phase 1, Phase 2 and Combined reviews. Phase 1 reviews lead to a determination in respect of each essential element that the essential element is: in place; in place, but certain aspects need improvement; or not in place. Phase 2 reviews lead to a rating of each of the essential elements along with an overall rating, applied on the basis of a four-tier system: Compliant; Largely compliant; Partially compliant; and Non-compliant. Both the Phase 1 determinations and the Phase 2 ratings are accompanied by recommendations for improvement.

Terms of Reference

I. Introduction

1. The Global Forum met on 1-2 September 2009 in Mexico and agreed in its Summary of Outcomes on a restructuring of the Global Forum and a three-year mandate to establish a robust and comprehensive peer review process to monitor and review progress made towards full and effective exchange of information.

2. In order to carry out monitoring and peer reviews, the Global Forum set up a Peer Review Group. The composition of the Peer Review Group was later agreed by the Global Forum and communicated by the chair to all members on 30 September. The Peer Review Group was mandated to "develop a methodology and detailed terms of reference for a robust, transparent and accelerated process" (see mandate in Annex 1).

3. The standards on transparency and exchange of information for tax purposes as developed by the Global Forum and the OECD are now almost universally agreed. The sources of the standards are described in Annex 2. The hallmarks of a good peer review system are open procedures coupled with a clear statement of the standards against which subjects are being reviewed. The terms of reference describe the standards and break them down into 10 essential elements to be assessed through the monitoring and peer reviews.

4. The terms of reference will be used by the assessment teams as the standards and key elements against which jurisdictions' legal and administrative framework and actual implementation of the standards will be assessed. They also served as a basis for the Secretariat to develop questionnaires that form the basis of the peer reviews. The questionnaires allow assessors to have a clear roadmap to conduct the peer reviews, which in turn will ensure that reviews are consistent and complete.

II. The Standards of Transparency and Exchange of Information for Tax Purposes

5. The principles of transparency and effective information exchange for tax purposes are primarily reflected in the 2002 OECD's Model Agreement on Exchange of Information on Tax Matters (the OECD Model TIEA) and its commentary and in Article 26 of the OECD Model Tax Convention on Income and on Capital (the OECD Model Tax Convention) and its commentary as updated in 2004 (and approved by the OECD Council on 15 July 2005). The revisions to Article 26 aimed at reflecting the work that the Global Forum has done have also been incorporated in the United Nations Model Double Taxation Convention between Developed and Developing Countries (the UN Model Tax Convention). The standards are now almost universally accepted. They were endorsed by the G20 Finance Ministers and Central Bank Governors at their meeting in Berlin in 2004. All members of the Global Forum have also now endorsed the standards.

6. The standards provide for exchange on request of foreseeably relevant information for the administration or enforcement of the domestic tax laws of a requesting party. Fishing expeditions are not authorised but all foreseeably relevant information must be provided, including bank information and information held by fiduciaries, regardless of the existence of a domestic tax interest or the application of a dual criminality standard.

7. In addition to the primary authoritative sources of the standards, there are a number of documents which have provided guidance in how the standards should be applied, in particular as regards transparency. For instance, in connection with ensuring the availability of reliable accounting information the Joint Ad Hoc Group on Accounts (JAHGA)[2] developed guidance on accounting transparency. Other secondary sources include the Manual on Exchange of Information (2006), the 2004 Guidance notes developed by the Forum on Harmful Tax Practices, and the FATF recommendations, standards and reports (see Annex 2).

---

2 The JAHGA was set up in 2003 under the auspices of the Global Forum. For the standards developed by the JAHGA see "Enabling Effective Exchange of Information: Availability Standard and Reliability Standard," (the JAHGA Report).

8. Exchange of information for tax purposes is effective when reliable information, foreseeably relevant to the tax requirements of a requesting jurisdiction is available, or can be made available, in a timely manner and there are legal mechanisms that enable the information to be obtained and exchanged.[3] It is helpful, therefore, to conceptualize transparency and exchange of information as embracing three basic components:

- availability of information
- appropriate access to the information, and
- the existence of exchange of information mechanisms

9. In other words, the information must be **available**, the tax authorities must have **access** to the information, and there must be a basis for **exchange**. If any of these elements are missing, information exchange will not be effective.

10. The remainder of this section breaks down the principles of transparency and effective exchange of information into their essential elements. In order for assessors to be able to evaluate whether a jurisdiction has implemented the standards or not, they will have to be in the position to understand each of the key principles and what a jurisdiction must do to satisfy that requirement. The sections are divided as discussed above into availability of information (Part A), access to information (Part B) and finally information exchange (Part C).

A. Availability of Bank, Ownership, Identity and Accounting Information

11. Effective exchange of information requires the availability of reliable information. In particular, it requires information on the identity of owners and other stakeholders as well as information on the transactions carried out by entities and other organisational structures. Such information may be kept for tax, regulatory, commercial or other reasons. If such information is not kept or the information is not maintained for a reasonable period of time, a jurisdiction's competent authority may not be able to obtain and provide it when requested.

3 JAHGA Report, para. 1.

A. Availability of Information – Essential Elements

A.1 Jurisdictions should ensure that ownership and identity information for all relevant entities and arrangements[4] is available to their competent authorities.

A.1.1. Jurisdictions[5] should ensure that information is available to their competent authorities that identifies the owners of companies and any bodies corporate.[6] Owners include legal owners, and, in any case where a legal owner acts on behalf of any other person as a nominee or under a similar arrangement, that other person, as well as persons in an ownership chain.[7]

A.1.2. Where jurisdictions permit the issuance of bearer shares they should have appropriate mechanisms in place that allow the owners of such shares to be identified.[8] One possibility among others is a custodial arrangement with a

---

4 The term "Relevant Entities and Arrangements" includes: (i) a company, foundation, Anstalt and any similar structure, (ii) a partnership or other body of persons, (iii) a trust or similar arrangement, (iv) a collective investment fund or scheme, (v) any person holding assets in a fiduciary capacity and (vi) any other entity or arrangement deemed relevant in the case of the specific jurisdiction assessed.

5 It is the responsibility of the jurisdiction under whose laws companies or bodies corporate are formed to ensure that ownership information in relation to those entities is available. In addition, where a company or body corporate has a sufficient nexus to another jurisdiction, including being resident there for tax purposes (for example by reason of having its place of effective management or administration there), that other jurisdiction will also have the responsibility of ensuring that ownership information is available.

6 OECD Model TIEA Article 5(4) (please note, however, exceptions for publicly-traded companies or public collective investment funds or schemes) and JAHGA Report paragraph 1. Note that FATF Recommendations state that jurisdictions should take measures to prevent the unlawful use of legal persons in relation to money laundering and terrorist financing by ensuring that their commercial, corporate and other laws require adequate transparency concerning the beneficial ownership and control of legal persons. Similar provisions apply to require adequate transparency concerning the beneficial ownership and control of trusts and other legal arrangements, as the case may be.

7 See B.1.1.

8 See footnote 3.

recognized custodian or other similar arrangement to immobilize such shares.

A.1.3. Jurisdictions should ensure that information is available to their competent authorities that identifies the partners in any partnership that (i) has income, deductions or credits for tax purposes in the jurisdiction, (ii) carries on business in the jurisdiction or (iii) is a limited partnership formed under the laws of that jurisdiction.[9]

A.1.4. Jurisdictions should take all reasonable measures[10] to ensure that information is available to their competent authorities that identifies the settlor, trustee[11] and beneficiaries of express trusts (i) created under the laws of that jurisdiction, (ii) administered in that jurisdiction, or (iii) in respect of which a trustee is resident in that jurisdiction.[12]

A.1.5. Jurisdictions that allow for the establishment of foundations should ensure that information is available to their competent authorities for foundations formed under those laws to identify the founders, members of the foundation council, and beneficiaries (where applicable), as well any other persons with the authority to represent the foundation.[13]

A.1.6. Jurisdictions should have in place effective enforcement provisions to ensure the availability of information, one

[9] OECD Model TIEA Article 5(4).

[10] The Global Forum will re-examine this aspect in light of the experience gained by jurisdictions in the context of the peer reviews and decide, before the end of Phase 1, if further clarifications are required to ensure an effective exchange of information.

[11] The term "trustee" as used herein shall be deemed to include a trust protector, administrator, and each other person (regardless of that person's applicable title with regard to the trust) who, under the terms of the trust and/or applicable law, has responsibility for the distribution and/or administration of the trust, whether or not that authority must be exercised in a fiduciary capacity, is shared with another person or persons, or is limited in its scope.

[12] OECD Model TIEA Article 5(4). See also commentary on express trusts in the appendix to the JAHGA Report, para. 6.

[13] OECD Model TIEA Article 5(4).

possibility among others being sufficiently strong compulsory powers.[14]

A.2 Jurisdictions should ensure that reliable accounting records are kept for all relevant entities and arrangements.[15]

A.2.1. Accounting records should (i) correctly explain all transactions, (ii) enable the financial position of the Entity or Arrangement to be determined with reasonable accuracy at any time and (iii) allow financial statements to be prepared.

A.2.2. Accounting records should further include underlying documentation, such as invoices, contracts, etc. and should reflect details of (i) all sums of money received and expended and the matters in respect of which the receipt and expenditure takes place; (ii) all sales and purchases and other transactions; and (iii) the assets and liabilities of the relevant entity or arrangement.

A.2.3. Accounting records should be kept for 5 years or more.

A.3 Banking information should be available for all account-holders.

A.3.1. Banking information should include all records pertaining to the accounts as well as to related financial and transactional information.[16]

B. Access to Bank, Ownership, Identity and Accounting Information

12. A variety of information may be needed in a tax enquiry and jurisdictions should have the authority to obtain all such information. This includes information held by banks and other financial institutions as well as information concerning the ownership of companies or the identity of interest holders in other persons or entities, such as partnerships and trusts, as well as accounting information in respect of all such entities.

---

14 FATF, AML/CFT Evaluations and Assessments: Handbook for Countries and Assessors, criteria 33.1-33.3, at p. 62 (April 2009).

15 See JAHGA Report.

16 See B.1.

13. Peer Review Group assessors shall determine if the access powers in a given jurisdiction cover the right types of persons and information and whether rights and safeguards are compatible with effective exchange of information.

B. Access to Information – Essential Elements

B.1. Competent authorities should have the power to obtain and provide information that is the subject of a request under an exchange of information arrangement from any person within their territorial jurisdiction who is in possession or control of such information (irrespective of any legal obligation on such person to maintain the secrecy of the information).[17]

B.1.1. Competent authorities should have the power to obtain and provide information held by banks, other financial institutions, and any person acting in an agency or fiduciary capacity including nominees and trustees, as well as information regarding the ownership of companies, partnerships, trusts, foundations, and other relevant entities including, to the extent that it is held by the jurisdiction's authorities or is within the possession or control of persons within the jurisdiction's territorial jurisdiction, ownership information on all such persons in an ownership chain.[18]

B.1.2. Competent authorities should have the power to obtain and provide accounting records for all relevant entities and arrangements.[19]

B.1.3. Competent authorities should use all relevant information-gathering measures to obtain the information requested, notwithstanding that the requested jurisdiction may not need the information for its own tax purposes (*e.g.*, information should be obtained whether or not it relates to a taxpayer that is currently under examination by the requested jurisdiction).

B.1.4. Jurisdictions should have in place effective enforcement provisions to compel the production of information.[20]

[17] See, however, section C.4.

[18] See OECD Model TIEA Article 5(4).

[19] See JAHGA Report paragraphs 6 and 22.

B.1.5. Jurisdictions should not decline on the basis of its secrecy provisions (*e.g.*, bank secrecy, corporate secrecy) to respond to a request for information made pursuant to an exchange of information mechanism.

B.2 The rights and safeguards (*e.g.* notification, appeal rights) that apply to persons in the requested jurisdiction should be compatible with effective exchange of information.

B.2.1. Rights and safeguards should not unduly prevent or delay effective exchange of information.[21] For instance, notification rules should permit exceptions from prior notification (*e.g.*, in cases in which the information request is of a very urgent nature or the notification is likely to undermine the chance of success of the investigation conducted by the requesting jurisdiction).

Exchanging Information

14. Jurisdictions generally cannot exchange information for tax purposes unless they have a legal basis or mechanism for doing so. The legal authority to exchange information may be derived from bilateral or multilateral mechanisms (*e.g.* double tax conventions, tax information exchange agreements, the Joint Council of Europe/OECD Convention on Mutual Administrative Assistance in Tax Matters) or arise from domestic law. Within particular regional groupings information exchange may take place pursuant to exchange instruments applicable to that grouping (*e.g.* within the EU, the directives and regulations on mutual assistance). Peer Review Group assessors will be tasked with determining whether the network of information exchange that a jurisdiction has is adequate in their particular circumstances.

C. Exchanging Information – Essential Elements

C.1. Exchange of information mechanisms should provide for effective exchange of information and should:

[20] See JAHGA Report paragraph 22.

[21] See OECD Model TIEA Article 1.

C.1.1. allow for exchange of information on request where it is foreseeably relevant[22] to the administration and enforcement of the domestic tax laws of the requesting jurisdiction.[23]

C.1.2. provide for exchange of information in respect of all persons (*e.g.* not be restricted to persons who are resident in one of the contracting states for purposes of a treaty or a national of one of the contracting states).

C.1.3. not permit the requested jurisdiction to decline to supply information solely because the information is held by a financial institution, nominee or person acting in an agency or a fiduciary capacity or because it relates to ownership interests in a person.[24]

C.1.4. provide that information must be exchanged without regard to whether the requested jurisdiction needs the information for its own tax purposes.[25]

C.1.5. not apply dual criminality principles to restrict exchange of information.

C.1.6. provide exchange of information in both civil and criminal tax matters.

C.1.7. allow for the provision of information in specific form requested (including depositions of witnesses and production of authenticated copies of original documents) to

---

22 See Articles 1 and 5(5) OECD Model TIEA and accompanying commentary. It is incumbent upon the requesting state to demonstrate that the information it seeks is foreseeably relevant to the administration and enforcement of its tax laws. Article 5(5) of the OECD Model TIEA contains a checklist of items that a requesting state should provide in order to demonstrate that the information sought is foreseeably relevant.

23 See Article 1 of the OECD Model TIEA, paragraph 5.4 of the Revised Commentary (2008) to Article 26 of the UN Model Convention and paragraph 9 of the Commentary to Article 26 of the OECD Model Convention.

24 OECD and UN Model Tax Conventions, Art. 26(5); OECD Model TIEA, Art. 5(4)(a).

25 OECD and UN Model Tax Conventions, Art. 26(4); OECD Model TIEA, Art. 5(2).

the extent possible under the jurisdiction's domestic laws and practices.

C.1.8. be in force; where agreements have been signed, jurisdictions must take all steps necessary to bring them into force expeditiously.

C.1.9. be given effect by the enactment of legislation necessary for the jurisdiction to comply with the terms of the mechanism.[26]

C.2 The jurisdictions' network of information exchange mechanisms should cover all relevant partners.[27]

C.3 The jurisdictions' mechanisms for exchange of information should have adequate provisions to ensure the confidentiality of information received.

C.3.1. Information exchange mechanisms should provide that any information received should be treated as confidential

---

26 OECD Model TIEA, Art. 10.

27 As agreed by the Global Forum's Sub-group on Level Playing Field issues in its paper Taking the Process Forward in a Practical Way (November 2008), a country is considered to have substantially implemented the standard of exchange of information for the purposes of this Global Forum assessment if it has in place signed agreements or unilateral mechanisms that provide for exchange of information to standard with at least 12 OECD countries. This benchmark was considered to be an appropriate dividing line at that point in time, between those countries that are implementing the standards and those that are not. However, this benchmark was recognised as part of a staged process and would have to be re-evaluated as circumstances evolved. In addition, in conjunction with the G20 Leaders' meeting in London on 2 April 2009, the Secretary-General of the OECD issued a progress report determining that a country that had signed agreements with 12 jurisdictions, whether OECD countries or other jurisdictions, would be considered to have substantially implemented the standard on exchange of information. It is apparent that for some jurisdictions, 12 agreements are likely to be too few to allow for exchange with all relevant requesting countries. Ultimately, the standard requires that jurisdictions exchange information with all relevant partners, meaning those partners who are interested in entering into an information exchange arrangement. Agreements cannot be concluded only with counterparties without economic significance. If it appears that a jurisdiction is refusing to enter into agreements or negotiations with partners, in particular ones that have a reasonable expectation of requiring information from that jurisdiction in order to properly administer and enforce its tax laws, this should be drawn to the attention of the Peer Review Group, as it may indicate a lack of commitment to implement the standards.

and, unless otherwise agreed by the jurisdictions concerned, may be disclosed only to persons or authorities (including courts and administrative bodies) concerned with the assessment or collection of, the enforcement or prosecution in respect of, or the determination of appeals in relation to, the taxes covered by the exchange of information clause. Such persons or authorities shall use the information only for such purposes.[28] Jurisdictions should ensure that safeguards are in place to protect the confidentiality of information exchanged.[29]

C.3.2. In addition to information directly provided by the requested to the requesting jurisdiction, jurisdictions should treat as confidential in the same manner as information referred to in C.3.1 all requests for such information, background documents to such requests, and any other document reflecting such information, including communications between the requesting and requested jurisdictions and communications within the tax authorities of either jurisdiction.

C.4 The exchange of information mechanisms should respect the rights and safeguards of taxpayers and third parties.

C.4.1. Requested jurisdictions should not be obliged to provide information which would disclose any trade, business, industrial, commercial or professional secret or information which is the subject of attorney client privilege or information the disclosure of which would be contrary to public policy.[30]

C.5 The jurisdiction should provide information under its network of agreements in a timely manner.

28 See Article 8 OECD Model TIEA; Article 26(2), OECD and UN Model Tax Conventions.

29 See B.2.

30 See OECD and UN Model Tax Conventions Article 26(3)(b) and commentary and OECD Model TIEA Article 7.

C.5.1. Jurisdictions should be able to respond to requests within 90 days of receipt by providing the information requested or providing an update on the status of the request.[31]

C.5.2. Jurisdictions should have appropriate organisational processes and resources in place to ensure timely responses.

C.5.3. Exchange of information assistance should not be subject to unreasonable, disproportionate, or unduly restrictive conditions.

III. Output of the Peer Review Process

15. For analytical purposes, it is important to distinguish the two phases in terms of their primary thematic scope. Phase 1 is concerned with a jurisdiction's legal framework and Phase 2 deals with the practical application of that framework. It is worth bearing in mind, however, that to the extent they are carried out sequentially Phase 2 would normally encompass to some degree the issues in Phase 1. Phase 2 reviews may also help clarify the significance of any shortcomings identified in Phase 1. Subsequent phases of peer review processes also typically review remedial efforts made by jurisdictions in response to issues identified in earlier review reports. This natural overlap between phases exists in other peer review systems, including the FATF and OECD Working Group on Bribery.

Phase 1 Reviews: The legal and regulatory framework

16. The Phase 1 review will assess each jurisdiction's legal and administrative framework against the essential elements. It will examine the jurisdiction's network of international agreements based on the information collected in the ongoing assessment of new agreements, updated as necessary. The review will also include situations where the treaty obligation may need to be incorporated into domestic law through legislation. The review will also verify that the absence of a domestic tax interest or the existence of strict secrecy provisions does not affect the ability to obtain and exchange information, and that domestic law provides for the relevant investigatory powers as appropriate. The availability of information in each jurisdiction will also be reviewed, including an appraisal of a jurisdiction's requirements to maintain accounting records against the JAHGA standards.

31 See Article 5(6)(b) of the OECD Model TIEA.

17. Accordingly, the report produced in connection with the Phase 1 review will include a detailed description of the elements of the jurisdictions' legal and administrative framework for transparency and exchange of information. This will be presented under 3 headings:

i) Availability of information

ii) Access to information

iii) Exchanging information

18. These sections would each be sub-divided between the essential elements described above. Some of the essential elements are susceptible to a yes or no determination following the Phase 1 review. In broad terms it will be possible to indicate whether a given jurisdiction has exchange of information arrangements with all relevant parties, if they have access to all relevant information and whether such information must in all cases be available. However, certain of the essential elements will require a Phase 2 review before any judgment can be made as to whether the jurisdiction satisfies the standard or not. In particular, whether the jurisdiction delivers information in a timely manner, and whether the rights and safeguards afforded persons in a jurisdiction unduly prevent or delay effective exchange of information will generally require an assessment of the practical application of a jurisdiction's legal framework for exchange.

19. In addition, the report will identify and describe any shortcomings that exist and provide recommendations as to how these might be addressed. Recommendations should be specific and provide clear guidance to the jurisdiction as to what is expected. To assist jurisdictions in implementing the standards the report may suggest a program of technical assistance where appropriate. In addition, the reviews may note that a jurisdiction engages in exchange of information practices that go beyond the standard, such as automatic or spontaneous exchanges of information, simultaneous examinations, or allowing representatives of the requesting jurisdiction to enter its territory to conduct interviews or examine records, or conduct such interviews or examine such records on behalf of another jurisdiction. This will not affect the assessment.

Phase 2: Monitoring and reviewing of the actual implementation of the standards

20. The second phase of the monitoring and peer review will focus on the effectiveness of exchange of information. Even if

satisfactory international instruments are in place together with a sound domestic legal framework, the effectiveness of exchange of information will depend on the practice of the competent authorities. Ultimately, the reviews will assess the quality of the information exchanged taking into account the views of the requesting parties.

21. There is a wide range of potential deficiencies, from lack of willingness to practical impediments such as insufficient resources to seek and exchange the required information or procedural requirements that frustrate effective exchange of information. There are also potential deficiencies in the quality of the requests made. Assessment of the effectiveness of the exchange of information requires quantitative data, such as statistics allowing meaningful review of the treatment of requests and the period between request and response, and qualitative data, indicating the reliability and relevance of the information exchanged to the requesting parties. Peer review should seek out input from a variety of sources, including at the on-site visit as appropriate, about the adequacy of the resources dedicated to achieving effective exchange of information.

22. The report on Phase 2 reviews will follow the same structure as in Phase 1, that is divided between exchange, access and availability of information. However, Phase 2 reviews will focus on the practical application in these areas and include an analysis of a jurisdictions' experience in information exchange. The assessments already made under Phase 1 could now be reviewed in light of the Phase 2 results. Where recommendations were provided following the Phase 1 review, these will be reviewed to determine whether they have been implemented. Where a jurisdiction generally performs satisfactorily in terms of providing the information requested within a reasonable time, then there will be little need to provide specific recommendations. However, where appropriate, recommendations will be made so that any potential difficulties in maintaining or achieving effective exchange of information can be avoided.

Annex 1 - Peer Review Group Mandate

The Summary of Outcomes agreed at the Global Forum meeting in Mexico on 1-2 September in relation to the establishing of a peer review process states:

(b) Establishing a robust and comprehensive monitoring and peer review process

- In order to carry out an in-depth monitoring and peer review of the implementation of the standards of transparency and exchange of information for tax purposes, the Global Forum agreed on the setting up of a Peer Review Group (PRG) to develop the methodology and detailed terms of reference for a robust, transparent and accelerated process.
- The terms of reference will be based on the proposals set out in the framework paper for more in depth monitoring and peer review as discussed at the meeting. There will be two phases for the peer review. Phase 1, which will examine the legal and regulatory framework in each jurisdiction, will begin early in 2010 and will be completed for all members within the initial three-year mandate. Phase 2, which will also begin early in 2010, will evaluate the implementation of the standards in practice. The Global Forum agreed that all members and relevant non-member jurisdictions will be covered by Phase 1 and Phase 2 reviews. The Peer Review Group will propose the scheduling of jurisdictions to be reviewed under Phase 2.
- Contrary to Phase 2 reviews, Phase 1 reviews would not normally require on site visits.
- In addition to the two phases of the peer review, the Global Forum will monitor legal instruments for exchange of information (*e.g.* double taxation treaties and tax information exchange agreements (TIEAs)). Such monitoring will now be continuous and cover both Global Forum members and relevant non-member jurisdictions, identifying and distinguishing between agreements in force and agreements signed but

not in force. It will focus on whether these agreements meet the standard. The first report is expected by December 2009.

- The Global Forum will continue to publish its annual updates and will issue the schedule of its upcoming reviews.

- The whole monitoring and peer review process will be an ongoing exercise. Evaluation reports will be published after adoption by the Global Forum. Jurisdictions will be expected to act on any recommendations in the review and to report back to the Global Forum on actions taken.

The Peer Review Group will develop more detailed guidance on how to implement these conclusions.

Annex 2 - Sources of the Internationally Agreed Standards on Transparency and Effective Exchange of Information for Tax Purposes (the Standards)

1. This annex briefly describes the authoritative sources setting out standards on transparency and effective exchange of information for tax purposes as well as additional sources that may be useful to assessors, the Peer Review Group and the Global Forum in applying the standards in the monitoring and peer review process. The internationally agreed standards on transparency and effective exchange of information for tax purposes may be divided into a primary authoritative source and a number of complementary elements.

2. The primary authoritative source contains:

- The 2002 Model Agreement on Exchange of Information on Tax Matters and its Commentary (Model Agreement);
- Article 26 of the OECD Model Tax Convention on Income and on Capital (Model Tax Convention) and its Commentary, which has now been incorporated in the UN Model Tax Convention;

3. This primary authoritative source is complemented by a number of secondary documents which give elements of context for the understanding and interpretation of the standards. These documents have been developed by the relevant OECD bodies or by the Global Forum. Finally, as work on standard-setting and evaluation closely relates to areas covered by other international bodies, and in particular the FATF, the principles developed by the FATF may be taken into consideration to interpret and apply the standards where appropriate.

I. Primary Authoritative Source

A. *Model Agreement and Commentary*

4. In 2002, the Global Forum created a Working Group on Effective Exchange of Information (the Global Forum Working Group). It included representatives from several OECD countries and Aruba, Bermuda, Bahrain, Cayman Islands, Cyprus, the Isle of Man, Malta, Mauritius, the Netherlands Antilles, the Seychelles and San Marino. The Working Group developed the 2002 Model Agreement which has been used as the basis for the negotiation of over 150 Tax Information Exchange Agreements (TIEAs).

5. The Model Agreement and Commentary is an authoritative source of the Global Forum standards on transparency and effective exchange of information for tax purposes. It addresses the standards for exchange of information in detail including with regard to the obligation to provide all information that is foreseeably relevant to the administration or enforcement of the domestic laws of the contracting parties concerning taxes, the narrow acceptable grounds for declining a request, the format of requests, confidentiality, attorney-client privilege and other matters.

6. The Model Agreement and Commentary also address the scope of information that must be available to be accessed and exchanged. The scope is primarily determined by the foreseeable relevance standard, *i.e.*, all information that is foreseeably relevant to the administration or enforcement of the domestic laws of the contracting parties concerning taxes.

7. In addition to establishing the general foreseeable relevance standard, the Model Agreement and Commentary identify specific types of information that the requested jurisdictions must have the authority to obtain and provide, including bank information and ownership and identity information.

8. The specific examples in the Model Agreement and Commentary are not exhaustive of the scope of information that must be available, accessible and reliable under the foreseeable relevance standard. They do not refer, for example, to accounting information. The scope of accounting information that is foreseeably relevant to the administration or enforcement of the domestic laws of the contracting parties concerning taxes is addressed specifically in the JAHGA paper (see below).

9. The Model Agreement and Commentary contains standards on access to information. For example, it provides that where the required review by the requested party of information in its possession proves inadequate to provide the requested information, it must take all "relevant

information gathering measures" in order to be able to provide the requested information.

10. The Model Agreement Commentary recognises that the standard it establishes can be implemented in several ways, including through double taxation agreements. Most double taxation agreements are based on the OECD Model Tax Convention.

B. Article 26 of the Model Tax Conventions and their Commentary

11. The Model Tax Convention is the most widely accepted legal basis for double taxation agreements. More than 3000 bilateral treaties are based on the Model Tax Convention. Article 26 of the Model Tax Convention in turn provides the most widely accepted legal basis for bilateral exchange of information for tax purposes.

12. In 2002, the OECD Committee on Fiscal Affairs (CFA) undertook a comprehensive review of Article 26 of the Model Tax Convention and its Commentary to ensure that they reflected current jurisdiction practices and to take account of the development of the Model Agreement by the Global Forum Working Group. In 2004, the current version of Article 26 and its Commentary was agreed and was first published in the 2005 version of the Model Tax Convention. The UN Committee of Experts on tax matters also incorporated the updated version of Article 26 in the UN Model Tax Convention. As of December 2009 the last reservations to Article 26 by Brazil and Thailand had been withdrawn.

13. Article 26 provides for the same standards as the Model Agreement. Both use the standard of "foreseeable relevance" to define the scope of the obligation to provide information. Both require information exchange to the widest possible extent, but do not allow "fishing expeditions", *i.e.* speculative requests for information that have no apparent nexus to an open inquiry or investigation.[32]

[32] The text of Article 26(1) was modified in 2005 to provide for the same basic "foreseeable relevance" standard as under the Model Agreement. The previous version of Article 26 used the standard of "necessary". The Commentary explains that the change from "necessary" to "foreseeably relevant" was not intended to alter the effect of the provision but was made to better express the balance between requiring information exchange to the widest possible extent while excluding fishing expeditions, and to achieve consistency with the Model Agreement. See Commentary paras. 4.1 and 5.

14. Although Article 26 is generally very similar in approach to the Model Agreement, some aspects of Article 26 are beyond the scope of the standards. For example, Article 26 allows for automatic and spontaneous exchange of information which is not included in the standard.

II. Complementary authoritative sources

A. The Joint Ad Hoc Group on Accounts (JAHGA) Report

15. Accounting information comes under the general foreseeably relevant standard established by the Model Agreement and Article 26 of the Model Tax Convention. However, the source of detailed standards with regard to the requirements for available, accessible and reliable accounting records is the JAHGA Report. Before being approved by the Global Forum in 2005, it was developed jointly by representatives of OECD and non-OECD countries through their cooperation in the JAHGA.[33]

16. The JAHGA Report sets out the standards with regard to requiring the maintenance of reliable accounting records, the necessary accounting record retention period and the accessibility to accounting records.

17. These apply to all "Relevant Entities and Arrangements", which are broadly defined to include (i) a company, foundation, Anstalt and any similar structure, (ii) a partnership or other body of persons, (iii) a trust or similar arrangement, (iv) a collective investment fund or scheme, and (v) any person holding assets in a fiduciary capacity (*e.g.* an executor in case of an estate). The JAHGA Report includes helpful explanatory notes on trusts and partnerships in an appendix.

B. The 2006 OECD Manual on Information Exchange

18. In 2006, the CFA approved a new Manual on Information Exchange (the Manual). The Manual provides practical assistance to officials dealing with exchange of information for tax purposes and may also be useful in designing or revising national manuals. It was developed with the input of both member and non-member countries of the OECD.

33 The JAHGA participants consisted of representatives from Antigua and Barbuda, Aruba, Bahamas, Bahrain, Belize, Bermuda, British Virgin Islands, Canada, Cayman Islands, Cook Islands, France, Germany, Gibraltar, Grenada, Guernsey, Ireland, Isle of Man, Italy, Japan, Jersey, Malta, Mauritius, Mexico, Netherlands, Netherlands Antilles, New Zealand, Panama, Saint Kitts and Nevis, Saint Lucia, Saint Vincent and the Grenadines, Samoa, Seychelles, Slovak Republic, Spain, Sweden, United Kingdom, and the United States.

19. The Manual follows a modular approach and some modules, such as the one on automatic exchange of information, are not relevant to the standards. However, two modules in particular provide useful guidance: the General Module on general and legal aspects of exchange of information and Module 1 on Exchange of Information on Request.[34]

C. The 2004 Guidance Notes developed by the Forum on Harmful Tax Practices

20. In 2004, the Forum on Harmful Tax Practices, a subsidiary body of the CFA, developed guidance notes on the issue of Transparency and Effective Exchange of Information.[35] The Introduction notes that the guidance notes, while providing useful guidance to jurisdictions that have made commitments to transparency and effective exchange of information, should not be understood as expanding the standards to which the jurisdictions had agreed to adhere (§ 13). The notes provide important guidance with regard to standards in the area of the availability of relevant and reliable information, including with regard to the identity of legal and beneficial owners and other persons.

D. FATF Recommendations, Standards and Reports

21. In addition to tax-specific materials addressed above, it is important to recognise that efforts to improve on transparency and effective exchange of information for tax purposes take place in a broader context. This is particularly the case with regard to the work of FATF relating to issues of domestic institutional measures to provide information, mutual legal assistance, and transparency with regard to information about ownership and the identity of owners and other stakeholders. These are key components of the foreseeably relevant information that jurisdictions must be able to provide under the Global Forum standards. FATF concepts may provide useful guidance and be taken into consideration to interpret and apply the standards where appropriate.

---

34 The Manual is available at *http://www.oecd.org/document/5/0,3343,en_2649_33767_36647621_1_1_1_1,00.html*

35 The guidance notes are available at *http://www.oecd.org/dataoecd/60/32/30901132.pdf*. They were published under the title Consolidated Application Note: Guidance in Applying the 1998 Report to Preferential Tax Regimes, and also addressed a variety of other preferential tax regimes. The notes on transparency and exchange of information are at pp. 9-19.

E. The 2008 Note on Taking the Process Forward and the 2009 Framework Note

22. The 2008 Note on Taking the Process Forward (para. 15) and the Framework Note (paras. 14-18) contain an important discussion of standards and issues relating to the assessment of progress made by jurisdictions in concluding new international agreements and the review of the relevance of those agreements. For example, they notably recognise that assessment of the number of agreements, including with regard to the benchmark of 12 agreements with OECD countries, (i) must be appreciated as part of a dynamic approach; (ii) should take account of the fact that bilateral agreements and their entry into force require action by both parties; and (iii) should record refusals to enter into agreements with partners, in particular ones of economic significance, because they may indicate a lack of commitment to implement the standards. Ultimately, the standard requires that jurisdictions exchange information with all relevant partners, meaning those partners who are interested in entering into an information exchange arrangement. Agreements cannot be concluded only with counterparties without economic significance.

F. Annual Assessments

23. The Global Forum has published annual assessments of the transparency and exchange of information regimes of many jurisdictions. They can be an important source of information about the standards and their implementation. The 2006 annual assessment report contains a summary of the standards and the annual assessments report generally on the application of the standards.

Revised Methodology for Peer Review and Non-Member Reviews

I. Introduction

1. The Global Forum at its 1-2 September 2009 meeting in Mexico decided to engage in a robust and comprehensive monitoring and peer review process. In order to carry out an in-depth monitoring and peer review of the implementation of the standards of transparency and exchange of information for tax purposes, the Global Forum agreed on the setting up of a Peer Review Group (PRG). The Global Forum agreed that the PRG would develop detailed terms of reference and the methodology for a robust, transparent and accelerated process.

2. As set forth in the Note 'Transparency and Exchange of Information for Tax Purposes: A Proposed Framework for In-Depth Monitoring and Peer Review, and for Restructuring the Global Forum' (Final Draft 27 August 2009), there are a number of general objectives and principles that govern Global Forum monitoring and peer review:

Effectiveness. The mechanism must be systematic and provide an objective and coherent assessment of whether a jurisdiction has implemented the standards.

Fairness. The mechanism must provide equal treatment for all members. Peer review of Global Forum members is an exercise among peers that can be frank in their evaluations. Reviews of non-members should be conducted only after a jurisdiction has been given the opportunity to participate in the Global Forum. The review process should provide the jurisdiction with an adequate opportunity to participate in its evaluation by the Global Forum.

Transparency. The mechanism will need to include a process for providing regular information to the public on the Global Forum work and activities and on implementation of the standards. This general responsibility must be balanced against the need for confidentiality which facilitates frank evaluation of performance.

Objectivity. The mechanism should rely on objective criteria. Jurisdictions must be assessed against the internationally agreed standards in accordance with an agreed methodology.

Cost-efficiency. The mechanism should be efficient, realistic, concise and not overly burdensome. It is necessary, however, to ensure that monitoring and peer review are effective, since together with the standards, they guarantee the level playing field. A high degree of procedural cooperation is necessary both for effectiveness and cost efficiency.

Co-ordination with other organisations. The mechanism should aim to avoid duplication of effort. Efforts should be made to use and take account of existing resources, including the Global Forum annual assessments and, where appropriate, relevant findings by other international bodies such as the FATF that engage in monitoring of performance in related areas.

3. This methodology sets forth procedures for the peer review of members and the equivalent review of non-members. It identifies the procedures and steps in the peer review process and additional procedures for reviews of non-members.[36]

4. Phase 1 will review the legal and regulatory framework for transparency and the exchange of information for tax purposes. Phase 2 will review the implementation of the standards in practice. Phase 2 reviews will necessarily encompass to some degree the issues in Phase 1 and may help clarify the significance of any shortcoming identified in Phase 1.

5. Combined Phase 1-2 reviews will encompass both review of the legal and regulatory framework (Phase 1) and the implementation of the standards in practice (Phase 2). Because they will generally involve on-site visits like Phase 2 reviews, the procedures for combined reviews will generally be similar to Phase 2 reviews. Except where otherwise specified, references to Phase 2 reviews herein apply to combined Phase 1-2 reviews accordingly.

---

36 Annex 3 summarises the key responsibilities of each of the participants in the review process. Annex 4 presents Model Assessment Schedules. Annex 5 presents a flowchart summarising the procedure for adoption of a report. Annex 6 is an outline of a peer review report.

6. The methodology sets out guidelines to conduct the peer reviews and the monitoring of non-members. They should be understood as guidelines rather than as rigid rules. The need to conduct fair, effective and transparent reviews should remain of paramount importance in applying the guidelines. The guidelines cannot and do not seek to address every possible contingency. The methodology in respect of Phase 1 is straightforward as it is based on a desktop review. As the Global Forum gains experience, particularly in respect of Phase 2 reviews, it is expected that the Phase 2 process will be modified or improved in the light of this experience, keeping in mind the need to ensure fairness and equal treatment.

II. Peer Reviews

A. *Creation of assessment teams and setting dates for evaluations*

7. Assessment teams will usually consist of two expert assessors, and these will be drawn primarily from PRG members coordinated by Secretariat staff, although GF members outside of the PRG will also be eligible to provide assessors. In selecting the assessors, account should be taken of the expertise and background of each assessor, the language of the evaluation, the nature of the legal system (civil law or common law), the specific characteristics of the jurisdiction (*e.g.* size and geographical location) and the need to avoid conflicts of interest. The team of assessors should include at least one person who is familiar with the nature of the legal system of the assessed jurisdiction, as well as one who can provide a different perspective. Assessors must be public officials drawn from relevant public authorities and should have substantial relevant experience of transparency and exchange of information for tax purposes. For Phase 2 reviews, assessors should also have had relevant practical experience with exchange of information for tax purposes.

8. The Secretariat will request each Global Forum member to designate a central point of contact to coordinate the identification of potential assessors to be recommended by the member. The designated central point of contact will be invited to supply name(s) and qualifications of potential assessor(s). Any designated central point of contact may be requested by the Secretariat to supply the name(s) and qualifications of assessor(s) that would be available for a particular review within seven days of the request being received. The chair and

vice-chairs of the PRG will issue a roster of assessors for the jurisdictions to be reviewed in the first six months. This will be distributed to the PRG for information only. Shortly afterwards, the chair and vice-chairs of the PRG will allocate these assessors to each of the jurisdictions for review during this period based on the criteria set out in paragraph 7. The PRG will be given 48 hours to comment on the proposal of the chair and vice-chairs of the PRG, with these comments to be taken into account to the extent possible. This process will be repeated for subsequent periods. The chair or a vice-chair, as the case may be, will not participate in the allocation of the assessors for the assessment of their own jurisdictions and the assessors for the assessments of those jurisdictions will be selected by the Peer Review Group, without the chair or vice-chair, as the case may be, of the PRG being present. Assessors will be provided with a handbook which will include the present note, the Terms of Reference and related source documents.

9. Each assessment team could participate in parallel in a number of reviews rather than in only one review. Coverage of multiple jurisdictions would provide each participating assessor with a stronger comparative perspective on each jurisdiction, while reducing the number of assessors required to incur costs to travel to the meeting.

10. The Secretariat will fix precise dates for the evaluation, consistent with the overall PRG schedule, in consultation with each jurisdiction and the assessors. The jurisdiction will advise whether it wishes to conduct the evaluation in English or French, and additional time for translation will be provided for as needed.

B. Obtaining input from jurisdictions' peers

11. Important to the process of peer review is the opportunity for other members of the Global Forum to provide their input into understanding the assessed jurisdiction's compliance with the standard. This applies both generally and more specifically to jurisdictions that have an exchange of information (EOI) relationship with the assessed jurisdiction.[37] Accordingly, members of the Global Forum will have two opportunities to provide input into the process of drafting the report by the assessors. The first opportunity for members to contribute will be prior to the commencement of the Phase 1 review

[37] In this regard, an EOI relationship should be understood to refer to one that meets the information exchange standards set forth in the Model Agreement on Exchange of Information on Tax Matters and in Article 26 of the OECD Model Tax Convention on Income and on Capital.

of a jurisdiction. At this point all Global Forum members will be invited to indicate any issues that they would like to see raised and discussed during the evaluation. The assessment team will take these issues into account in developing appropriate questions for the review.

12. Prior to the commencement of the Phase 2 review members with an EOI relationship with the assessed jurisdiction will be invited to provide comments again. An important part of Phase 2 is the cross-checking of the views of the assessed jurisdiction about its implementation of the international standards with the views of jurisdictions with which it has an EOI relationship. The credibility of the Global Forum's work relies on the active involvement of all its members to provide for an accurate and relevant picture of how the assessed jurisdiction's EOI system works in practice. It is thus essential to have substantial input from jurisdictions that have EOI experience with the assessed jurisdiction.

13. A questionnaire (the "Peer Questionnaire") will be sent to each Global Forum member jurisdiction that has an EOI relationship with the assessed jurisdiction. The Peer Questionnaire will have a standard format and will require various inputs on the quality of information exchange. It will elicit information about how active the EOI relationship is, the type of information exchanged, *e.g.* bank, ownership and accounting information and the timeliness and quality of responses. It will also seek information about the difficulties, if any, that the requesting jurisdiction has faced in obtaining information from the assessed jurisdiction as well as information about positive experiences. The assessed jurisdiction can request that other jurisdictions be invited to provide input as well.

14. Partner jurisdictions should provide their responses to the questionnaire to the Secretariat within 3 weeks. While Peer Questionnaires will be sent to all Global Forum members with an EOI relationship with the assessed jurisdiction there is an increased responsibility on those jurisdictions that have a significant EOI relationship with the assessed jurisdiction to respond to it.[38] While ensuring that confidentiality is preserved, partner jurisdictions should be specific and provide as much detail as possible to aid the assessment team and assessed jurisdiction in their efforts to analyse and evaluate the difficulties encountered. Issues or concerns

[38] In this regard, a significant EOI relationship should be understood to mean, at a minimum, having made or received more than two information exchange requests to the assessed jurisdiction within the previous three years.

previously raised by the assessed jurisdiction to the partner jurisdiction in relation to its requests should also be described by the partner jurisdiction.[39] Responses will be made available to the assessment team and to the assessed jurisdiction.

15. The assessment team will analyse the peer input to identify issues and to develop appropriate questions for the assessed jurisdiction to allow it to respond to any concerns. These questions should be sent to the assessed jurisdiction concurrently with the formal issuance of the standard Phase 2 questionnaire (see below). In assessing responses to the Peer Questionnaire, the assessment team should take into account the nature of the EOI relationship and the degree of detail provided by the partner jurisdiction.

16. Documents produced by Global Forum members concerning an assessed jurisdiction (*e.g.* responses to the questionnaire, proposed questions for the assessed jurisdiction, and responses by the assessed jurisdiction) will be treated as confidential and will not be made publicly available.[40]

17. Because peer review is an intergovernmental process, business and civil society groups participation in the formal evaluation process and in particular, in the evaluation exercise and the discussions in the PRG or Global Forum is not foreseen. The publication of the schedule of upcoming reviews would enable business and civil society groups to provide information or opinions if they so wish.

39 For example, if a partner jurisdiction is aware that the assessed jurisdiction is concerned about a lack of confidentiality or lack of reciprocity on behalf of the partner jurisdiction, it should make such issues known, so that the review may proceed more expeditiously.

40 To ensure appropriate confidentiality with respect to the Peer Questionnaire, prior to circulation of a report to the PRG, a partner jurisdiction that is explicitly or implicitly identified in the text of the draft report will be given the opportunity to review and comment upon any text in the report that explicitly or implicitly identifies that partner jurisdiction. The partner jurisdiction will be given the opportunity to request changes that allow its identity to remain anonymous from the PRG and the public (although not the assessment team or the assessed jurisdiction, which will have seen earlier drafts of the report).

C. Getting responses from the assessed jurisdiction to the questionnaire

18. From the perspective of the assessed jurisdiction, the first step in the review is the receipt of a questionnaire from the Secretariat. The questionnaire for the assessed jurisdiction will have a standard format. It will generally be supplemented by jurisdiction-specific questions. These may include questions regarding specific institutions or procedures in the assessed jurisdiction, issues raised by other Global Forum members (see above) and (in the case of a Phase 2 review) issues arising from an earlier Phase 1 report.

19. The standard questionnaire for Phase 2 will include requests for quantitative data allowing meaningful review of the treatment of requests and the period between request and response, and qualitative data in order to help assess the reliability and relevance of information provided to the requesting parties. It will also allow the assessed jurisdiction to comment on the quality of requests it receives.

20. Combined reviews will similarly use a standard questionnaire that encompasses both the standard Phase 1 and Phase 2 questionnaires. Jurisdiction-specific questions will also generally be used.

21. The questionnaire format is designed to facilitate the preparation of a focussed and relevant response. Jurisdictions should provide a detailed description (and analysis where appropriate) of the relevant measures and actions, including appropriate citations from supporting laws or other material.

22. All necessary laws, regulations, guidelines and other relevant documents should be available in the language of the evaluation and the original language (unless otherwise agreed with the assessment team), and both these documents and the responses to the questionnaire should be provided in an electronic format. The time required for translation of documents must be taken into account by the jurisdiction under review. Where English or French is not the native language of the assessed jurisdiction, the process of translation of relevant laws, regulations and other documents should start at an early stage.

23. Documents produced by an assessed jurisdiction during a review (*e.g.* documents describing a jurisdiction's regime, responses to the questionnaire, or responses to assessors' queries) and by the Secretariat or assessors (*e.g.* reports from assessors, draft reports, etc.) will be treated as confidential and should not be made publicly

available, unless the assessed jurisdiction and the Secretariat consent to their release. Strict respect of the confidentiality of the work is a must for the credibility of the process. Any breach of the confidentiality of the process shall be brought to the attention of the PRG Chair and vice-Chairs, who shall decide on the most appropriate action, in consultation with the PRG as appropriate.

24. The assessed jurisdiction should provide its responses to the questionnaire (and any additional questions) within a maximum of 4 weeks of receipt of the questionnaire for Phase 1 and Phase 2 reviews, and within a maximum of 6 weeks for combined reviews.[41]

25. Phase 2 reviews contain additional steps relating to the on-site visit (detailed immediately below). For the next steps in a Phase 1 review, see below the section on Completing the draft report for the PRG.

D. The on-site visit

26. On-site visits are an important aspect of the Phase 2 reviews. They provide the assessed jurisdiction with an opportunity to participate more fully in its evaluation and allow an open, constructive and efficient dialogue between the assessed jurisdiction and the assessment team. Face-to-face dialogue will help avoid misunderstandings and improve the quality of the resulting draft report, and ultimately may avoid the need for an oral discussion at the PRG. It will also focus high level government attention on any existing deficiencies in jurisdiction's practices in the area of transparency and exchange of information. In exceptional cases, where the assessment team considers that an on-site visit would serve no useful purpose, the assessment team should present its views in writing to the members of the PRG. If there is no objection within 1 week and the assessed jurisdiction agrees, then the on-site visit will be dispensed with.

a) Timing

27. Each Global Forum member jurisdiction agrees to allow an on-site visit of approximately 2-3 days, or longer as appropriate, for the purpose of providing information from a variety of sources concerning its law and practice with regard to the issues covered by

41 For the first reviews supplementary questions may be prepared while the assessed jurisdiction is answering the standard questionnaire.

the Phase 2 evaluation. The schedule should provide for the on-site visit taking place after the receipt of the responses to the questionnaire.

b) The agenda for the on-site visit

28. The primary goal of the on-site visit should be to obtain evidence required to evaluate the assessed jurisdiction's overall effectiveness in exchanging requested information. The on-site visit should be carried out in accordance with an agenda programme agreed between the assessed jurisdiction and the assessment team, taking account of the specific requests expressed by the team. The agenda should be finalised by the assessed jurisdiction at least one week before the on-site visit.

29. The focus will be primarily on the assessed jurisdiction's competent authority and all of the agencies and entities with which it may interact in the process of responding to information requests. The nature of the discussions will depend on the legal and regulatory institutions and policies of the assessed jurisdiction. Discussions should encompass both potential areas of weaknesses and of best practices in all areas covered by the standards, as set forth in the terms of reference. Assessors must be thoroughly familiar with the terms of reference and the note on assessment criteria.

E. Compiling Information for the Phase 2 Review

30. Typical areas of investigation that assessors would consider include the following:

- The degree to which in practice information is maintained and by whom.
- The practical application of the jurisdiction's compulsory powers to obtain information.
- The timeliness of the jurisdiction's responses in relation to different types of requests for information, *e.g.* bank, ownership and accounting information, and any factors contributing to delays in response times.
- The comprehensiveness of the jurisdiction's exchange of information program.

- The adequacy of the organisational structure and resources having regard to the exchange of information demands made on the jurisdiction.
- The practical application of the jurisdiction's rules regarding the confidentiality of information exchanged.

31. In order to engage in the cross-checking that is at the core of the Phase 2 process, the circumstances involved in cases where the exchange of information process was seen as unsatisfactory by requesting jurisdictions should be explored. This may require consultation with requesting jurisdictions, in particular cases, to ensure that requests have been properly framed. Because of the confidentiality of tax information, however, the assessment team will not have access to the actual requests for information and the responses from the requested jurisdiction.[42] It is recognised that the confidentiality of information that identifies a specific taxpayer is a fundamental principle of the standards and jurisdictions' domestic laws.

F. Completing the draft report for the PRG

32. Phase 1 reports are initially drafted after receipt of responses to the questionnaire. Taking account of the initial views of the assessors with regard to the responses to the questionnaire, the Secretariat will turn the questionnaire responses into an initial draft report within 4 weeks following the receipt of the responses.

33. Phase 2 reports are initially drafted after the on-site visit. Following the on-site visit, the Secretariat will prepare a draft Phase 2 report in 4 to 6 weeks.

34. The Secretariat will cross-check other Global Forum assessments to ensure consistency of evaluation across reports. The initial draft reports on the assessed jurisdictions will be provided to the assessors for review and the assessors will be expected, as much as possible, to independently cross-check the reports against other assessments of the Global Forum in order to ensure consistency across assessments. The assessment team may ask additional questions to the assessed jurisdiction during the course of drafting.

42 The PRG will explore the possibility of developing provisions for jurisdictions to allow access to non-identifying information in certain cases.

35. The additional steps in finalising a draft report prior to a PRG meeting, and the approximate time that is required for each step, are as follows (see also Annex 4):

i. Assessors to provide comments on the draft reports to the Secretariat (maximum 2 weeks).

ii. Secretariat to revise the draft reports in light of the assessor comments. Draft report to be sent to the assessed jurisdiction (maximum 1 week).

iii. Jurisdiction to provide comments to the Secretariat (maximum 4 weeks in Phase 1 or 2; maximum 6 weeks for combined reviews), which are forwarded to the assessors for their views. The report will reflect the comments of the assessed jurisdiction on the weaknesses that have been identified and its plans to address them. Within this time, the assessment team will also have prepared the draft executive summary, provided it to the jurisdiction for comment (for at least 1 week) and received the jurisdiction's comments. The draft executive summary should contain key findings briefly describing the key risks, the strengths and the weaknesses of the system, and any overarching recommendations made to improve it.

iv. Assessment team to review and decide on the changes that need to be made to the draft reports (maximum 2 weeks).

36. It is important to note that the assessors and the jurisdiction need to respect the timetables, since delays may significantly impact the ability of the PRG to discuss the report in a meaningful way. By agreeing to participate in the review process, the jurisdiction and the assessors undertake to meet the necessary deadlines and to provide full and accurate responses, reports or other material as required under the agreed procedure.

37. Where there is a failure to comply with the agreed procedure, the assessment team can recommend action and refer the matter to the PRG chair and vice-chairs. The following examples illustrate the types of actions that could be taken:

i. Failure by the jurisdiction to provide a timely or sufficiently detailed response to the questionnaire or additional questions in the eyes of the assessment team could lead to the deferral of the review, and the PRG chair may write to the head of delegation or the relevant Minister in the jurisdiction. The PRG is to be advised as to reasons for deferral so that it may consider appropriate action.

Where appropriate, the assessment team, consulting with the PRG chair and vice-chairs will indicate to the jurisdiction that it considers that a Phase 1 review involving an exceptional on-site visit would be appropriate to facilitate the collection and evaluation of information.

ii. Upon a failure by the jurisdiction to provide a timely response to the draft report, the chair may write a letter to the head of delegation or the relevant Minister in the jurisdiction. Where the delay results in a report not being discussed, the PRG is to be advised of the reasons for deferral so that it may consider appropriate action, including with regard to disclosure of the name of the jurisdiction.

38. Throughout the review, the assessed jurisdiction and the assessment team should take all reasonable steps to resolve any differences or difficulties to avoid where possible the need for an oral debate in the PRG (see below) or to assist the PRG in its work. If differences or difficulties still remain, they will be highlighted by the Secretariat in a cover note to the draft report which will be submitted to the PRG along with the draft report and a note by the assessed jurisdiction documenting the outstanding issues it has with the draft report, in order to facilitate the examination of the report by the PRG members.

G. Circulation of the report to the PRG and the PRG meeting

a. Circulation of the report to the PRG for comments

39. The Secretariat will send the draft reports and executive summaries to all PRG members at least five weeks prior to the PRG meeting for comment.

40. A number of reports may be suitable for PRG approval under a written procedure. Such procedure will be followed when there is agreement between the assessment team and the assessed jurisdiction on the content of the report. Under this procedure, if no comments or objections by any members are received within three weeks, the report is considered to be approved by the PRG.

41. Only draft reports that have not been approved under the written procedure will be discussed orally during the PRG meeting. PRG members making comments or objections should explain clearly the basis for their comments or objections so that the assessment team

and the assessed jurisdiction have a proper appreciation of them. The comments or objections on all reports will be sent to the PRG members at least seven days prior to the meeting.

42. The assessment team, in consultation with the assessed jurisdiction, will try to address comments or objections received. The Secretariat will circulate any amended draft reports including editorial adjustments and substantive comments the assessment team considered appropriate as early as possible and at the latest seven days before the meeting. Outstanding issues will be highlighted by the Secretariat in a cover note to the revised draft report which will be submitted to the PRG, along with the draft report, and a note by the assessed jurisdiction documenting the outstanding issues it has with the draft report. Such a note by the assessed jurisdiction should be supported by copies of relevant legislation or other supporting materials that have not already been provided previously to the assessors.

a. PRG meeting

43. The procedure for the discussion of the draft report and the executive summary (including a set of key findings) at the PRG meeting will be as follows:

44. During the first reading:

i. Assessment team introduces itself, and the assessors present in high-level terms the key issues from the report, the amendments made to integrate the PRG's written comments, and the substantive outstanding issues. The team will have the opportunity to intervene/comment on any issue concerning the report.

ii. Assessed jurisdiction makes its opening statement, also addressing the substantive outstanding issues. Additional editorial changes should not be discussed orally but provided to the Secretariat.

iii. The PRG then discusses the issues raised in the report, focusing on the substantive outstanding issues. As a matter of good practice, delegations should not raise comments that they have not raised in writing. However, should a delegation wish to bring up a new issue, it should, if possible, inform the PRG/Secretariat in advance of the discussion. The PRG should give careful consideration to the views of the assessors and the jurisdiction when deciding on the wording, as well as taking into account the need to ensure consistency between reports.

45. Once the first reading is complete, the assessment team, first in consultation with the assessed jurisdiction, will incorporate any amendments agreed by the PRG into the draft. A revised version of the report will then be circulated as a room document.

46. A second reading will take place at the same PRG meeting:

i. Assessment team presents the revised version of the report and summarises any changes made to the draft report to reflect the discussions of the first reading.

ii. Assessed jurisdiction has an opportunity to respond to the changes it disagrees on.

iii. The PRG then discusses the revisions made after the first reading with a view to approving the revised report.

iv. The report and the executive summary are approved when consensus of the PRG is reached.[43]

47. The approved report is a report of the PRG for submission to the Global Forum, and not simply a report by the assessors.

48. Review reports may include an annex (Annex 1) emphasising recent changes made to the assessed jurisdiction's EOI framework or EOI mechanisms or presenting future plans which impact on transparency and exchange of information for tax purposes. This annex also presents the jurisdiction's response to the review report and shall not be deemed to represent the Global Forum's views. The assessed jurisdiction should draft the annex within one week of the approval of the report by the PRG.

49. When consensus could not be reached at the PRG meeting, the text of the report is not approved. The PRG will task the assessment team in consultation with the assessed jurisdiction to revise the report, which will then be dealt with under the procedures set out in paragraphs 39-48 above. If the revised report is not approved through written procedure, the next PRG meeting will discuss only those issues on which consensus was not reached in the first meeting. The assessed jurisdiction will be invited to participate in this meeting.

50. If the approval of a report is not obtained after two consecutive meetings of the PRG, the report shall be presented to the Steering Group for consideration and inclusion in the agenda of the next Global Forum meeting for oral debate. The Steering Group must

---

43 Consensus in the context of the approval or adoption of a report means that no one jurisdiction can block the approval of the report.

take a decision in the week following the PRG meeting at which the report failed to obtain approval.

H. Procedures following the PRG meeting: review and adoption of the report by the Global Forum

51. When the report has been approved by the PRG, it will be circulated to the Global Forum together with Annex 1 within one week. In case the annex has not been finalised, the text will be circulated to the Global Forum without the annex, which will be circulated when ready, at the latest prior to the adoption of the report. Members of the Global Forum will be invited to adopt the report under written procedure. In the absence of any objections within three weeks, the report is considered to be adopted. If there are objections, the Steering Group of the Global Forum shall decide whether to refer the report back to the PRG for consideration at its next meeting or to include discussion of the report in the agenda for the next Global Forum meeting. In these cases, the assessed jurisdiction will have an opportunity to update Annex 1 to reflect substantial changes in the jurisdiction's EOI framework that occurred in the meantime, but not later than two weeks before the next meeting where the report will be discussed.

52. The Global Forum shall use an approach to consensus that ensures that no one jurisdiction can block the adoption or publication of a review. Nevertheless, every effort should be made to arrive at a consensus and the views of the jurisdiction would be fully noted. The discussions and consultations in the Global Forum are open to Global Forum members and observers. Only Global Forum members, however, will take part in the adoption of the report and evaluation.

I. Publication of reports

53 Transparency is an important principle of Global Forum peer reviews. Regular information should be provided to the public on the Global Forum work and on implementation of the standards. After each report has been adopted by the Global Forum, it shall be made public by the Secretariat on the Global Forum website.

54. In the exceptional circumstance that the Global Forum fails to adopt a report, the public will be provided with an explanation for the absence of a report in order to maintain the credibility of the Global Forum process. The text of the explanation will be in a standard format agreed by the Global Forum and will identify the

issue(s) at stake and the jurisdictions that object to the draft report. This text would be circulated to the Steering Group and the jurisdictions concerned two days in advance of putting it on the Global Forum website.

J. Follow-up

55. It is important to follow-up assessments and recommendations included in a report and to publicly acknowledge progress that has been made since the assessment was made. As a matter of course, Phase 2 reports will evaluate and report on any post-Phase 1 changes in relevant legislation or policy in the assessed jurisdiction. In some cases, however, where significant changes have been made by a jurisdiction prior to the publication of its Phase 2 report, it is important to note the changes more quickly, in a supplementary report, prepared by the assessment team, which will revise the assessment made of a jurisdiction, as set below. There also needs to be a mechanism for the Global Forum to publicise significant post-Phase 2 changes.

a) Peer review follow-up procedure

56. In all cases a formal follow-up procedure is necessary to ensuring that reports are properl y followed up by assessed jurisdictions. In addition, peer review reports may be quickly outdated as jurisdictions might implement quickly the recommendations made. Where changes introduced by a jurisdiction would result in a need to revise the determinations included in a report because the element could be considered in place, it is critical that a supplementary report is drafted and submitted to the Global Forum for adoption. The issue of a jurisdiction lowering its level of commitment or back stepping its legal and regulatory framework or practice of EOI should also be addressed.

57. First, within one year of the Global Forum's adoption of a review report, the assessed jurisdiction shall provide a detailed written report to the PRG of the steps it has taken or is planning to take to implement any recommendations, for the PRG's review and evaluation. In addition, the assessed jurisdiction will provide an intermediary report within six months of the Global Forum's adoption of its report if that report determines that at least one essential element is "not in place". It will also provide any additional report that has been requested by the review report.

58. Second, at any time after the Global Forum's adoption of a report, when the assessed jurisdiction implements changes that are likely to result in an upgrade in a determination of an essential element to "the element in place", the assessed jurisdiction can inform the chair of the PRG and submit a detailed written report for the PRG to consider, clearly indicating why the change justifies a revision of the determination, and ask for a supplementary report to be prepared. The presumption is that six months should elapse from the adoption of a report by the Global Forum before a supplementary report is submitted to the PRG but an earlier submission would be possible if the PRG Chair and vice-chairs agree that there are special circumstances justifying this.

59. Third, if substantial changes occur in a jurisdiction but none of the possibilities on formal follow-up above are activated, for instance where a jurisdiction back steps its legal and regulatory framework or stops exchanging information, the Chair of the PRG can ask the jurisdiction to present the changes to the PRG, and the PRG may decide to launch a follow-up procedure.

60. In all cases, inputs will be sought from Global Forum members and the PRG will take note of the changes reported and may decide to propose to the Global Forum to revise the recommendations and determinations based on a supplementary report prepared by the assessment team (see below).

61. A supplementary report will be prepared as follows:

- The assessed jurisdiction provides a detailed written report to the assessment team of the steps it has taken to implement the recommendations or other substantial changes that have occurred.
- The assessment team (assessors and Secretariat) undertakes an analysis in consultation with the assessed jurisdiction and, from 4 to 6 weeks following the receiving of the jurisdiction's written report, prepares a detailed supplementary report to assess the changes made (or not) in the jurisdiction. In the event that the assessment team proposes to revise any of the determinations, the supplementary report will include a revised summary of determinations and recommendations. If a jurisdiction has not corrected its deficiencies, the assessment team may propose that a further follow-up procedure be decided.

- The PRG considers and approves the assessment team's supplementary report by written procedure. The assessment team's report is sent to the PRG at least five weeks prior to the next meeting of the PRG which will consider the report in line with existing approval procedure for peer review reports in paragraphs 39-50.
- Amendments approved by the PRG will be immediately submitted to the Global Forum for adoption through written procedure, in accordance with the procedure in paragraphs 51-52.
- The adopted supplementary report will be made public on the Global Forum website, in accordance with the procedure in paragraphs 53-54, alongside the original report. The original report itself will not be revised since it reflects the situation at a particular time.

62. Given the time that may elapse between the adoption of the report and the preparation of a supplementary report, the original assessors may no longer be available to prepare the supplementary report. In the event that an original assessor is not available, or no longer qualifies as an assessor under paragraph 7, the Secretariat will liaise with the central point of contact, in the member jurisdiction that provided the assessor, to identify a successor.

b) Ongoing monitoring

63. As decided by the Global Forum at its September 2009 meeting in Mexico, the Global Forum will be continuously monitoring legal instruments for exchange of information in each jurisdiction, including those not yet reviewed. In connection with this continuous monitoring, the Secretariat will also be able to note significant factual post-report developments while indicating that they have not been reviewed or evaluated by the Global Forum, on its public website. A website link to such a factual update report will be provided in connection with the Global Forum's annual assessment.

III. Procedures for Reports on Non-Members

64. Reviews of non-members of the Global Forum will occur in a manner similar to reviews of members to the greatest extent possible except as otherwise provided hereunder.

A. Selection of non-members for review

65. The purpose of review of non-members is to prevent jurisdictions from gaining a competitive advantage by refusing to implement the standards or participate in the Global Forum.

66. The PRG should discuss any issues with regard to non-members on a regular basis. It can make a proposal to the Steering Group for approval of the review of a non-member and seek approval of the Global Forum under the written procedure. The PRG should ensure that all Global Forum members are invited to identify appropriate non-members for review.

67. Prior to a review commencing, the non-member jurisdiction should be informed about the possibility of becoming a member of the Global Forum if the jurisdiction commits to implement the standards, accepts to be reviewed and pays the membership fee.

B. Participation of non-members in their review by the Global Forum

68. Non-members who do not seek to become members will generally be given the same opportunity to participate in their review as Global Forum members, including the opportunity to organise an on-site visit. However, while participation should be encouraged, it is important that the report be prepared using the best available information even if the assessed jurisdiction is not cooperative. Non-members do not participate in the formation of consensus.

69. In the event the invitation to agree to an on-site visit is not accepted or the jurisdiction otherwise fails to cooperate with the review process, the PRG may also consider other appropriate action.

IV. Funding

70. The budget of the Global Forum will bear the expenses for the travel and per diem expenses for the members of the Secretariat who are part of assessment teams.

71. The members taking part in the evaluations as assessor jurisdictions will bear the costs of travel and per diem expenses for their experts assigned to assessment teams. Each PRG member should expect to provide 2-3 assessors over the course of the first mandate.

72. The assessed jurisdiction will bear the cost of replying to the questionnaire, translating all relevant materials as well as interpretation costs and defraying the travel and per diem expenses of experts who attend the PRG and Global Forum meetings to present the jurisdiction's views on the report. The assessed jurisdiction will also bear the costs to organise the on-site visit (other than the travel and per diem expenses for the assessors and members of the Secretariat as addressed above). The jurisdiction would also be invited to bear the costs for any delay in the process for which it is responsible.

Annex 3 – Summary of the Key Responsibilities of Participants in a Review

This annex summarises the key responsibilities of participants in Phase 1, Phase 2 and combined Phase 1-2 reviews. Because the procedures for combined reviews will generally be similar to Phase 2 reviews, references to Phase 2 reviews herein also apply to combined reviews except where otherwise specified.

I. RESPONSIBILITIES OF SECRETARIAT

A. *Assessment Schedule:* In accordance with the overall schedule adopted by the Global Forum, the Secretariat establishes, in consultation with the assessors and the assessed jurisdiction, a schedule of the steps of each individual review.

B. *Assessment Team:* Secretariat staff coordinates the assessment team.

C. *Questionnaire and Supplementary Questions:* The Secretariat reviews the assessed jurisdiction's annual assessment, inputs from GF members and additional materials, and prepares a list of additional questions to supplement the standard questionnaire(s). In Phase 2 reviews, specific questions may also relate to issues arising from an earlier Phase 1 review. The supplemental questions are sent to the assessed jurisdiction after consultation with the assessors.

D. *On-site visit (for Phase 2 and combined reviews):* in consultation with the assessors and the assessed jurisdiction, the Secretariat prepares the agenda.

E. *Preparation of Report and Supplementary Report:*

1. Pre-PRG Discussion: The Secretariat coordinates the drafting of a report which incorporates the assessors' views. It is then provided to the assessed jurisdiction. The Secretariat, in consultation with the assessors, makes any appropriate changes in response to comments and corrections submitted by the assessed jurisdiction. The report reflects the comments of the assessed jurisdiction and its plans to address the weaknesses identified.

2. PRG and Global Forum meetings: As part of the assessment team, the Secretariat will have the opportunity to intervene or comment on issues concerning the report.

3. Post-meetings: After the PRG approval of a report, the Secretariat will be responsible for editing and transmitting the report to the Global Forum. After a Global Forum adoption of a report, the Secretariat will be responsible for publishing the report.

II. RESPONSIBILITIES OF ASSESSORS

A. *General.* Each jurisdiction that agrees to provide an assessor, and each individual assessor that accepts such a role, fully accepts all of the obligations relating to such service, including the provision of timely comments, participation in on-site visits, and full attendance at all possible meetings (preparatory, PRG and if necessary Global Forum). Jurisdictions that are not able to carry out their obligations should notify the Secretariat without delay to allow another assessor jurisdiction to be chosen. The PRG shall be notified if the Secretariat is unable to find a substitute assessor and will decide on how to proceed. Assessors are bound by a confidentiality duty and cannot share documents related to the review they are performing outside the assessment team.

B. *Appointment of Assessors*. The steps below should be followed:

1. Once a Global Forum member has indicated that it is prepared to provide assessors, it should designate a central point of contact and, if possible, provide a list of the names and qualifications of potential individual assessors. Assessors should be public officials drawn from relevant public authorities. Assessors for Phase 2 and combined reviews should also have relevant practical experience with actual exchange of information for tax purposes. Potential assessors receive a handbook compiling the relevant documents.

2. Global Forum members providing assessors are informed by the Secretariat, with as much notice as possible, of the decision of the chair and vice-chairs of the PRG about the jurisdictions their assessors will be asked to review, and the dates for the reviews.

3. The Global Forum members will inform the Secretariat of any reasons why they consider it would not be appropriate for them to be involved in reviewing one or more of the jurisdictions selected.

4. The assessed jurisdiction will inform the Secretariat of any reasons why it considers that it would not be appropriate for a particular jurisdiction to be part of the assessment team.

5. The Global Forum members providing assessors propose, through their central point of contact, which of their individual potential assessors could undertake the review and should supply the name and qualifications of the prospective assessors to the Secretariat within seven days from the receiving of a Secretariat request.

C. *Composition of Assessment Team.* The assessment team which usually consists of two expert assessors as a whole should include experts in areas relevant to the issues presented by a specific jurisdiction's examination, *e.g.* interpretation of tax treaties, statutes, regulations and practices including in the areas of international exchange of information; accounting and transparency issues; and access to information. The assessors may consult with each other to ensure that there is adequate coverage of relevant issues. A jurisdiction may nominate two assessors for combined Phase 1-2 reviews. Individuals serving as assessors have a duty to assess objectively, in their personal capacity.

D. *Written Review.* The assessors:

1. Work with the Secretariat to develop a list of supplementary questions.

2. Identify issues raised by the assessed jurisdiction's response to the questionnaire and communicate these issues to the Secretariat for inclusion in follow-up questions or incorporation into the draft report.

3. Work with the Secretariat in the preparation of the report.

E. *On-site Visit (for Phase 2 and combined reviews):* assessors participate in all aspects of the on-site visit, and substantively contribute to the discussions during the on-site meeting with the assessed jurisdiction as well as during the preparatory and debriefing discussions with the Secretariat.

F. *Supplementary reports*: the assessors analyse the contents of the written report submitted by the assessed jurisdiction and work with the Secretariat to prepare a short note or supplementary report.

G. *PRG and Global Forum Meetings.* The assessors attend, as necessary, the PRG meeting to present the draft report and any Global Forum meetings that discuss the report in depth.

III. RESPONSIBILITIES OF THE ASSESSED JURISDICTION

A. *Central Point of Contact.* The assessed jurisdiction designates a central point of contact who is responsible for ensuring that communications with the Secretariat are forwarded promptly to the relevant persons in the assessed jurisdiction and for ensuring the confidentiality of the documents related to the review process within the assessed jurisdiction.

B. *Questionnaire and Supporting Materials.* In accordance with the schedule established by the Secretariat, the assessed jurisdiction submits a written response to the questionnaire and supplemental questions, as well as supporting materials, including summaries of relevant cases.

1. Although it is preferable that these answers be integrated into a single written response, the assessed jurisdiction should not delay providing a response for that purpose. Further, if the answers to specific questions are not complete by the deadlines set in the assessment schedule, the assessed jurisdiction should submit such answers as are complete and supplement its response as needed.

2. The assessed jurisdiction provides supporting materials, such as laws, regulations, and judicial decisions. It is essential that all materials be provided on a timely basis to allow the assessors and the Secretariat to review them. Supporting materials should be provided in English or French, as well as in the original language unless otherwise agreed with the Secretariat. Where the materials are voluminous, the assessed jurisdiction should discuss with the Secretariat which items should be translated on a priority basis.

3. The assessed jurisdiction also answers any additional follow-up questions, triggered by its answers to the questionnaire.

C. *On-site Visit*

1. The assessed jurisdiction provides access to relevant officials as required in the agenda, in consultation with the Secretariat and the assessors. The names, titles, and responsibilities of each participant are provided to the Secretariat in advance of the on-site visit. The assessed jurisdiction should do its utmost to ensure that the list of participants reflects the proposals of the assessment team.

2. The assessed jurisdiction is responsible for providing a venue for the on-site visit.

3. Although the assessed jurisdiction is not required to make travel arrangements for the assessment team, it may consider negotiating for hotel rooms at a government rate at a location convenient to the venue of the meetings.

4. The language (English or French) in which the assessment will be conducted is agreed upon in advance. The assessed jurisdiction may be required to provide interpretation and translation as deemed necessary by the assessment team.

D. *The Draft Report*

1. The assessed jurisdiction should carefully review the draft report and submit any corrections or clarifications it deems appropriate, indexed to specific paragraphs of the draft report. This should not be viewed as an opportunity to rewrite the report.

2. Comments must be submitted within the time limits set in the assessment schedule. To ensure that the PRG receives the draft report in time to review it prior to the PRG meeting, comments that are submitted late will not be included in the draft report circulated to the PRG but will be circulated separately.

3. When a draft report is discussed orally during a PRG meeting, the assessed jurisdiction may present its views.

E. *Post-Review.* Within six months and/or one year of the Global Forum's adoption of the Report, or at any other time when so requested pursuant to paragraphs 55-62, the assessed jurisdiction shall provide an intermediate/detailed written report of what steps it has taken or is planning to take to implement the recommendations. In addition if, at any time after the Global Forum's adoption of a report, the assessed jurisdiction implements changes that are likely to result in an upgrade in a determination of an essential element to "the element is in place" it can submit a detailed written report and request a review of the relevant determination.

IV. RESPONSIBILITIES OF PRG MEMBERS AND GLOBAL FORUM MEMBERS

A. *Providing Input for Phase 1 Reviews*: Global Forum members are invited to indicate any issues they would like to see raised and discussed during the evaluation.

B. *Questionnaire for Phase 2 Reviews*: Global Forum members with an exchange of information relationship with the assessed jurisdiction are invited to fill-in a questionnaire on the quality of information exchange, and to indicate any issues they would like to see raised and discussed during the evaluation. Those jurisdictions that have a significant exchange of information relationship with the assessed jurisdiction have a particular responsibility to respond to the questionnaire within the assigned deadline. Global Forum members who have filled-in the questionnaire should be ready to answer possible follow-up questions from the assessment team.

C. *Comments on Draft Reports:* PRG and Global Forum members ensure that a qualified expert(s) reviews the draft reports, and provides, as need be, comments on requests for written approval or adoption. PRG and Global Forum members respect the confidentiality of all documents related to the review process.

D. *Follow-up to Reviews:* PRG members ensure that a qualified expert(s) reviews the follow-up reports prepared by the assessed jurisdiction and assessment team, and provides comments, objects or raises questions, as need be.

E. *Attendance at PRG Meetings:* PRG members ensure the attendance of a qualified expert(s) at each PRG meeting. Absences should be notified one week in advance of the meeting. PRG members who fail to attend three successive meetings will be automatically removed from the PRG, and the Global Forum will elect a new member.

Annex 4 –Model Assessment Schedules

Phase 1 Review

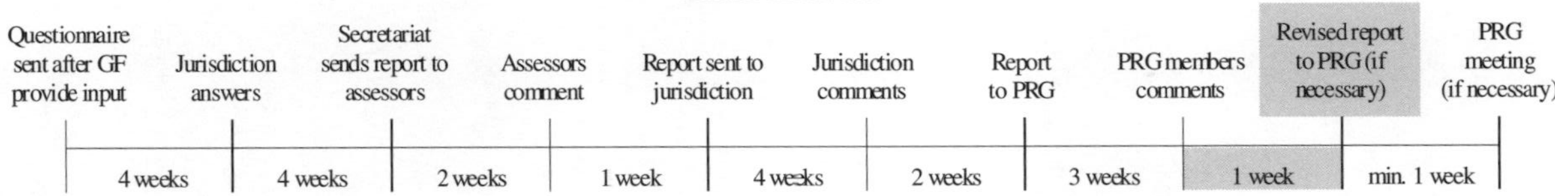

Phase 2 Review

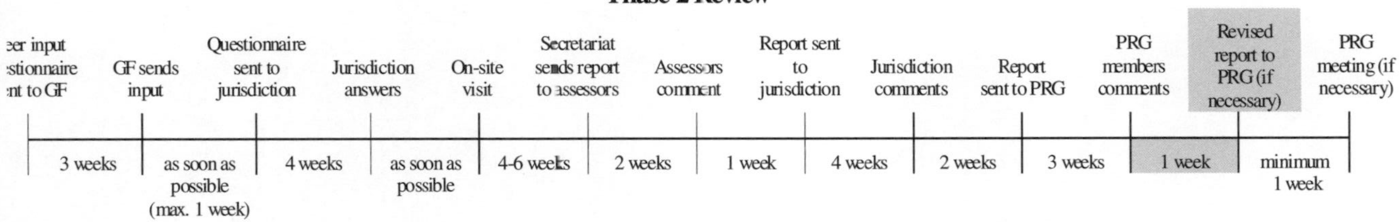

Combined Phase 1-2 Review

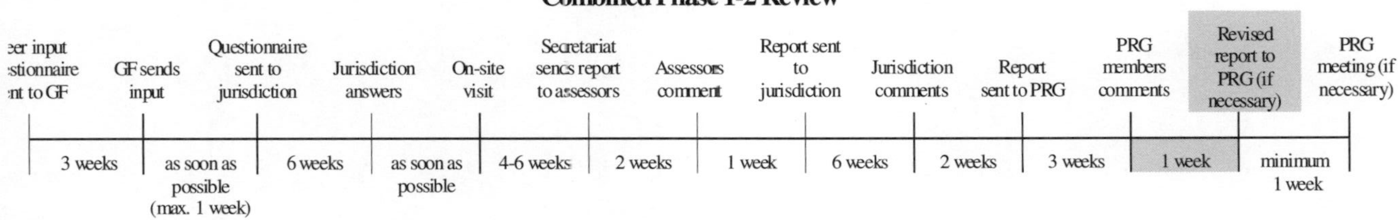

Annex 5 – Chart on the Procedure to Adopt Reports

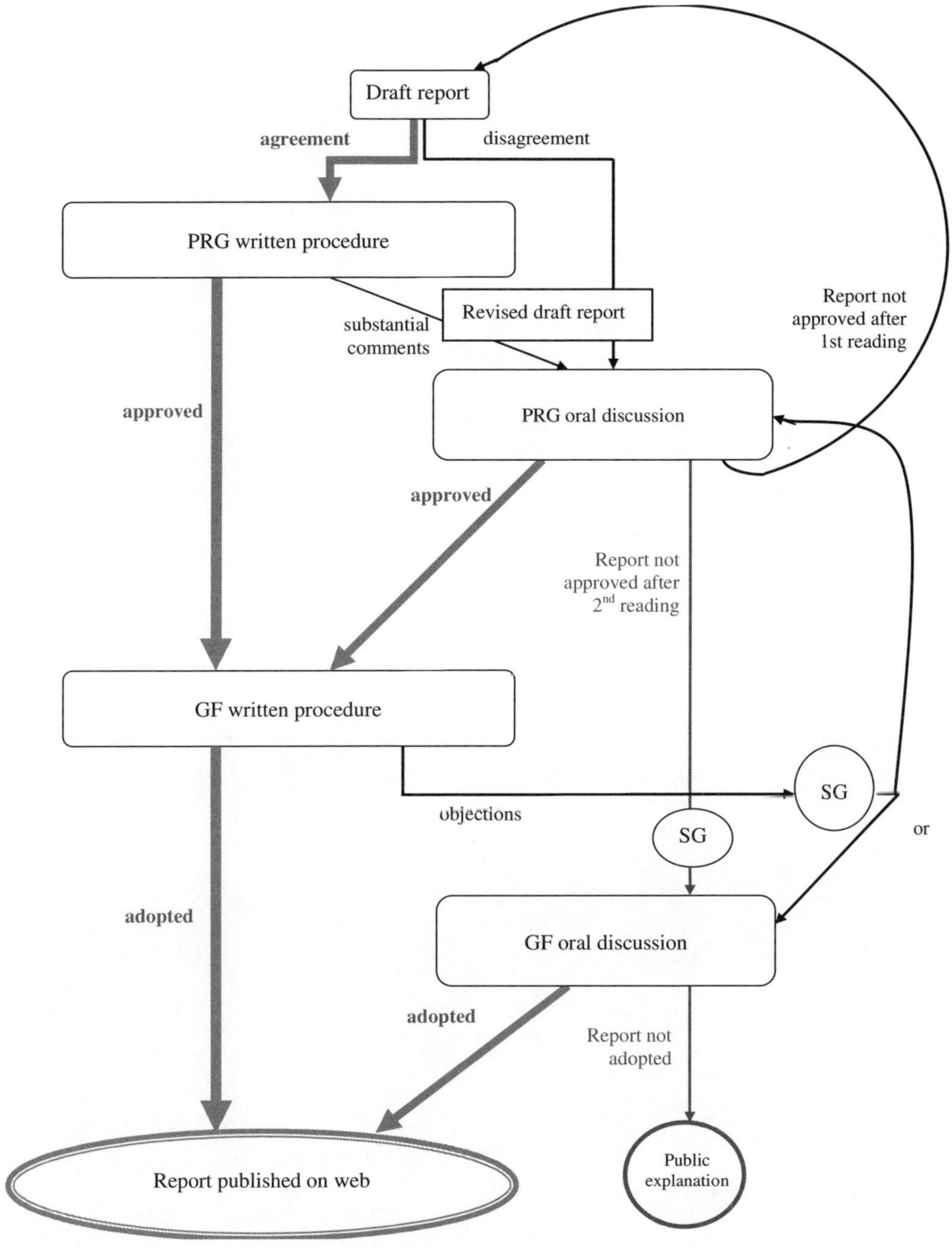

Annex 6 – Outline of Peer Review Report

The present annex provides initial guidance with regard to the outline for peer review draft reports (for Phase 1, Phase 2 and combined reports) to be prepared by the assessment team for approval by the PRG (and subsequent adoption by the Global Forum). As assessment teams and the PRG gain experience, the outline may be modified in future. Draft reports should as much as possible follow a similar presentation and have a similar length and level of details, even though each report will be tailored to the individual jurisdiction being assessed.

Executive Summary (1-2 pages)

1. Introduction (approximately 3-6 pages)

A. Presentation of the monitoring exercise and information specific to the review (for example identification of the assessors, logistical information, organisation or not of an on-site visit).

B. Overview of the assessed jurisdiction – this sub-section identifies relevant elements of the jurisdiction's political, economic and legal system. It also summarises the history of the jurisdiction's involvement with exchange of information and the Phase 1 report, where relevant.

C. Recent developments – this sub-section briefly presents any recent actions taken by the assessed jurisdiction to implement the standards (before they are individually analysed in Section 2).

2. Compliance with the standards (Approximately 15-30 pages)

This section will be divided into three sub-sections. Each sub-section will then generally be divided into its essential elements as described in the Terms of Reference and provide a detailed analysis of the jurisdiction's compliance with each essential element:

A. Availability of information

1. A.1. Ownership and identity information

2. A.2. Accounting records; etc.

B. Access to information

C. Exchange of information

In Phase 2 and combined reports, the analysis should focus in particular on those issues identified in the Phase 1 report or by other Global Forum members – either generally or through the special questionnaire filled in by members that have an exchange of information relationship with the assessed jurisdiction.

In all reports, the assessed jurisdiction's compliance with the essential elements will be evaluated and recommendations for remedial action will be made where relevant. The opinion of the assessed jurisdiction will also be reflected in the report, as well as its planned actions to implement any recommendations made.

3. **Summary of assessments and recommendations** (1-2 pages)

This section includes a table that compiles the jurisdiction's assessment for each essential element and their possible associated recommendation(s). The report concludes with the presentation of the next steps for the jurisdiction in the peer review process, including a timetable for providing follow-up reports to the PRG.

Assessment Criteria

Introduction

1. The Terms of Reference note breaks down the standards of transparency and exchange of information into 10 essential elements under three broad categories: (A) availability of information; (B) access to information; and (C) exchanging information. This note establishes a system for assessing the implementation of the standards that corresponds to the Global Forum's goals of achieving effective exchange of information and to the subject and structure of the review process for both Global Forum members and non-members. Briefly, Phase 1 reviews will lead to an assessment of the jurisdictions' legal and regulatory framework, accompanied where necessary by recommendations for improvement. Phase 2 reviews will assess the application of the standards in practice, along with recommendations related to all of the categories, and will ultimately lead to a rating of each of the essential elements along with an overall rating. This note must be read in conjunction with the Terms of Reference and Methodology notes.[44]

The Goal of the Rating System

2. The object of the Global Forum's review process is to promote universal, rapid and consistent implementation of the standards of transparency and exchange of information. This can be achieved when international tax co-operation allows tax administrations to effectively

44 See Terms of Reference to Monitor and Review Progress Towards Transparency and Exchange of Information for Tax Purposes CTPA/GFTEI(2009)1/REV2 and Methodology for Peer Reviews and Non-Member Reviews CTPA/GFTEI(2009)2/REV2.

administer and enforce their tax laws regardless of where their taxpayers choose to locate their assets or organise their affairs.

3. The Global Forum's annual reports already show that the legal and regulatory frameworks in place today are not equivalent among all jurisdictions. Internationally, there is a broad variation in the level of implementation of the standards. The progress made by a jurisdiction in implementing the standards, and likewise a failure to make such progress, should be highlighted as part of the Global Forum's review process. In this context the Global Forum reviews should:

- give recognition to progress that has been made,
- identify areas of weakness and recommend remedial actions so that jurisdictions can improve their legal and regulatory frameworks as well as their exchange of information practices, and
- identify jurisdictions that are not implementing the standards.

4. The assigning of a rating is only one of the components of the review process relevant to achieving these goals. Recommendations setting out clearly what improvements a jurisdiction needs to make and, where possible, obtaining the agreement and commitment of the reviewed country to the recommendation(s) are especially important. Indeed, ratings will always be assigned in light of such recommendations. In order to act as an incentive for jurisdictions to follow recommendations and respond to ratings given by the Global Forum, however, the system should be dynamic and capable of taking into account developments as they occur. While the Peer Review Group and ultimately the Global Forum may not be in a position to re-evaluate jurisdictions immediately each time they make changes to their systems of exchange of information, there should be an effective system of on-going monitoring that is flexible enough to respond to a fast-changing environment. In accordance with the Methodology note, the PRG will consider and elaborate proposed procedures for re-evaluating jurisdictions in light of changes that they make to their systems for the exchange of information.

5. The review process is intended to be dynamic with the Global Forum continually monitoring the process as the reviews proceed. Jurisdictions will want to review the recommendations that are addressed to other jurisdictions to see if these are relevant for them.

The Structure of the Rating System

Rating of the essential elements

6. The review process is divided into two phases, one that addresses the legal and regulatory framework that is in place in a jurisdiction and one that addresses the effectiveness of the implementation of the standards in practice. As noted, the standards are divided among 3 broad categories and are broken down into 10 essential elements. The essential elements themselves are further broken down into 31 enumerated aspects. A rating system could therefore take on a number of structures. It is possible to rate each element and enumerated aspect during both Phase 1 and Phase 2, to rate only essential elements and/or to give an overall rating. Each aspect of the review process should be evaluated in the manner which best fulfils the objectives set out above and that promotes an efficient operation of the review process.

7. There are a number of reasons why it would not be appropriate to rate each enumerated aspect. Not all of the enumerated aspects are relevant to all jurisdictions, whereas there may be cases of certain considerations that are so specific to a particular jurisdiction that they are not directly covered by a specific enumerated aspect within an element of the Terms of Reference. The same enumerated aspect may also have different significance in different cases. Even if the enumerated aspects are not rated *per se*, they will each have to be evaluated by the assessment team. Recommendations made by the assessment team will be as specific as possible and so will generally be directed to the enumerated aspects. In light of these considerations, the enumerated aspects of the elements will not be given a rating *per se* in the reports provided to the PRG. This will allow the PRG (and the Global Forum) to focus their efforts on the main substantive issues, rather than expending excessive time in discussions of individual ratings, and ensure that where PRG delegates require further information, this will be contained in the commentary of the report, or may be presented by the assessment team during oral debate.

Outcomes of Phase 1 reviews

8. A distinction should be drawn between Phase 1 and Phase 2, and between the respective types of assessment that should be applied to each of them. Phase 1 reviews are concerned with the adequacy of a legal and regulatory framework for the exchange of information and so they evaluate what is a necessary but not sufficient condition for the *effective* exchange of

information. Phase 2 reviews consider the effectiveness of the transparency and exchange of information practices in a jurisdiction and thus these reviews can reveal whether and to what degree a jurisdiction is in compliance with the international standards. Consequently, the purpose of a Phase 1 review is to assess the extent to which a jurisdiction has in place the elements that would allow it to achieve effective exchange of information in practice. For this reason it would be inappropriate to assign definitive ratings at the end of Phase 1, although whether a jurisdiction moves to its Phase 2 review will depend on the outcome of the Phase 1 review.

9. Accordingly, Phase 1 assessments will lead to one of the following determinations in respect of each essential element:

Determinations – Phase 1
The element is in place
The element is in place, but certain aspects of the legal implementation of the element need improvement
The element is not in place

These determinations will be accompanied by recommendations for improvement.

10. A jurisdiction will normally qualify for a Phase 2 review once its Phase 1 review has been completed, even if certain aspects of the elements are identified as requiring some improvements. Jurisdictions would normally have strengthened their legal and regulatory frameworks where required in accordance with Phase 1 recommendations. If so, these improvements would be assessed in the context of the Phase 2 review. Where improvements have not been made, this will also have an impact on the Phase 2 outcome.

11. In cases where a jurisdiction does not have in place elements which are crucial to it achieving an effective exchange of information in its particular case, the jurisdiction will not move to a Phase 2 review until it has acted on recommendations to achieve an improved legal and regulatory framework.[45] Each case may be different, and may require individualized

45 Jurisdictions chosen for combined reviews are from among those with established systems of exchange of information and experience with its practice. Where the Phase 1 aspects of the combined review indicate that elements which are crucial to the jurisdiction achieving an effective exchange of information are not in place, this should be brought to the

attention from the PRG, but a very clear example of such a circumstance would be a jurisdiction that does not have in place an agreement with any relevant jurisdiction that provides for the exchange of information in tax matters or a jurisdiction that has no access to bank or ownership information or where reliable accounting information generally is not available. If the PRG concludes that the jurisdictions' legal and regulatory framework does not allow for effective exchange of information and as a result the Phase 2 review is deferred, then the position will be reviewed on the occasion of the jurisdiction's detailed written report to the PRG within 12 months of the adoption of the report. Once the jurisdiction has sufficiently addressed the recommendations made in the Phase 1 report, then its Phase 2 review shall be scheduled.

Outcomes of Phase 2 reviews

12. In contrast to Phase 1, it is appropriate in the context of a Phase 2 review to provide ratings of the jurisdiction's compliance with the standards, as the effectiveness of implementation of the essential elements can be rated once an appropriate subset of jurisdictions has been assessed. Through the Phase 2 reviews, jurisdictions will have the opportunity to demonstrate (whether through quantitative data or other factors) that implementation of the essential elements is effective in practice.

13. While each of the essential elements will be rated, the ultimate object of the exercise is to evaluate the overall effectiveness in practice of a jurisdiction's system for exchange of information. The issuance of an overall rating will best achieve both the recognition of progress by jurisdictions toward the level playing field and the identification of jurisdictions that are not in step with the international consensus.

14. The Phase 2 evaluation, including the overall rating, would be applied on the basis of a four-tier system:

attention of the PRG chair and vice-chairs to determine whether an adjustment to the schedule of reviews should be made.

Rating	Phase 2 – Exchange of Information
Compliant	The essential element is, in practice, fully implemented.
Largely compliant	There are only minor shortcomings in the implementation of the essential element.
Partially compliant	The essential element is only partly implemented.
Non-compliant	There are substantial shortcomings in the implementation of the essential element.

Application of the Rating System

15. Peer reviews and non-member reviews require informed judgements to be made by the assessors and the members on the basis of the information provided to them. Jurisdictions must implement the international standards in a manner consistent with their national legislative and institutional systems, and so the methods by which compliance is achieved may differ from jurisdiction to jurisdiction. What is essential is that a jurisdiction is able to respond to a request for information in a manner that enables the exchange of information to be effective. Responsibility for ensuring a fair and consistent outcome of the reviews as a whole and the application of the rating system in particular will fall to the PRG, which should have an active role in ensuring that similar cases are treated similarly and that real distinctions in the effectiveness of the systems for the exchange of information in different jurisdictions are reflected in the assessments given to each. Of course, the assessment teams will play a crucial role in this regard as they will be charged with crafting the draft report for approval of the PRG.

16. In determining the ratings for the essential elements in Phase 2 reviews, assessors must exercise judgment in terms of whether shortcomings in the implementation of an essential element are minor or substantial, and how such shortcomings translate into ratings in a four-tier system. In coming to this determination, assessors must ultimately evaluate what impact the shortcomings have on effective exchange of information. This can include an appraisal of the extent to which the impediment was cited by the jurisdictions' exchange of information partners, or whether the type of information or request concerned relates to a large portion of the

jurisdiction's flows of income or investment. For example, a jurisdiction may have a deficiency in providing information in practice in respect of companies that have issued bearer shares, but only allow the issuance of such shares in limited circumstances and the jurisdiction's exchange of information partners have not cited this as a significant problem. In such a case this may be regarded as a shortcoming that would not, on its own,[46] lead to a determination that the jurisdiction is only Partially or Largely Compliant in respect of element C.1.

17. It is also important to note that assessors will already have considered the impact that a shortcoming has on the jurisdiction's practical ability to exchange information when formulating their recommendations. Assessors should ensure that the classification of a shortcoming as minor or not is consistent with the tenor of the recommendations issued in connection with it. It would be unusual if a particular shortcoming is regarded as minor, but its remedy required the jurisdiction to take quite serious and involved steps to remedy it. For example, if assessors determine that a jurisdiction has an inadequate infrastructure for exchange of information and have made a recommendation for significant and wholesale changes, then this should correspond to more than a minor shortcoming in the practical exchange of information. Conversely, if assessors do not uncover significant difficulties in the jurisdiction's practical experience with exchange of information, then this should impact the urgency of the recommendation regarding the jurisdiction's infrastructure.

18. While the overall rating will be based on a global consideration of a jurisdiction's compliance with the individual essential elements, this cannot be a purely mechanical approach. This will require judgment, taking into account the outcomes from the Phase 1 and Phase 2 reviews and the manner in which jurisdictions have responded to any recommendations made. In particular, the Compliant category should not be viewed as an unobtainable goal that requires perfection as consideration must be given to the fact that some jurisdictions engage in extensive exchange of information including in a variety of sophisticated cases, whereas others may be limited to delivering information on a much more limited scale. This judgment must take into account the nature, complexity and scale of information requests made to the jurisdiction.

19. It will be important to complete Phase 2 reviews for a subset of jurisdictions representing a geographic and economic cross-section of the

46 Whether a series of shortcomings amounts to a deficiency that would lead to a determination that the jurisdiction is only Partially or Largely Compliant will depend on the individual circumstances.

Global Forum before finalising ratings, in order to ensure that application of the ratings system is consistent across jurisdictions. This is because the ratings determination is likely to require some comparative perspective, without which early ratings may not be consistent. Thus, the publication of ratings should be taken up by the Peer Review Group and ultimately the Global Forum at such time as a representative subset of Phase 2 reviews is completed, which would be expected to be within the first mandate.[47] In the interim, to ensure that the work of the Global Forum progresses expeditiously and promotes rapid and consistent implementation of the standards, both Phase 1 and Phase 2 reports will be published with full assessments as they are adopted by the Global Forum.

Conclusion

20. A variety of considerations have an impact on the choices made in designing an assessment system, from theoretical and substantive factors to practical concerns inherent in any undertaking of this nature. Ultimately, the goal is to create a system that can be fairly and efficiently applied and which encourages continuing progress towards effective exchange of information across a broad universe of jurisdictions each having its own unique characteristics. The assessment system balances these factors against the objectives of the assessment system. Phase 1 reviews assess jurisdictions' legal and regulatory framework coupled with recommendations for improvement for the essential elements in categories A (availability of information), B (access to information) and C (exchanging information). Phase 2 reviews will include recommendations related to all of the categories, and be accompanied by ratings for each of the essential elements, as well as an overall rating, as soon as a representative subset of reviews is completed.

47 The PRG will review the question of when ratings should be assigned and advise the Steering Group, which in turn would consult the Global Forum.

PART II: MAIN SOURCES OF STANDARDS

Article 26 of the OECD Model Tax Convention on Income and on Capital and its Commentary

ARTICLE 26

EXCHANGE OF INFORMATION

1. The competent authorities of the Contracting States shall exchange such information as is foreseeably relevant for carrying out the provisions of this Convention or to the administration or enforcement of the domestic laws concerning taxes of every kind and description imposed on behalf of the Contracting States, or of their political subdivisions or local authorities, insofar as the taxation thereunder is not contrary to the Convention. The exchange of information is not restricted by Articles 1 and 2.

2. Any information received under paragraph 1 by a Contracting State shall be treated as secret in the same manner as information obtained under the domestic laws of that State and shall be disclosed only to persons or authorities (including courts and administrative bodies) concerned with the assessment or collection of, the enforcement or prosecution in respect of, the determination of appeals in relation to the taxes referred to in paragraph 1, or the oversight of the above. Such persons or authorities shall use the information only for such purposes. They may disclose the information in public court proceedings or in judicial decisions.

3. In no case shall the provisions of paragraphs 1 and 2 be construed so as to impose on a Contracting State the obligation:

a) to carry out administrative measures at variance with the laws and administrative practice of that or of the other Contracting State;

b) to supply information which is not obtainable under the laws or in the normal course of the administration of that or of the other Contracting State

c) to supply information which would disclose any trade, business, industrial, commercial or professional secret or trade process, or information, the disclosure of which would be contrary to public policy (ordre public).

4. If information is requested by a Contracting State in accordance with this Article, the other Contracting State shall use its information gathering measures to obtain the requested information, even though that other State may not need such information for its own tax purposes. The obligation contained in the preceding sentence is subject to the limitations of paragraph 3 but in no case shall such limitations be construed to permit a Contracting State to decline to supply information solely because it has no domestic interest in such information.

5. In no case shall the provisions of paragraph 3 be construed to permit a Contracting State to decline to supply information solely because the information is held by a bank, other financial institution, nominee or person acting in an agency or a fiduciary capacity or because it relates to ownership interests in a person.

COMMENTARY ON ARTICLE 26

CONCERNING THE EXCHANGE OF INFORMATION

I. Preliminary remarks

1. There are good grounds for including in a convention for the avoidance of double taxation provisions concerning co-operation between the tax administrations of the two Contracting States. In the first place it appears to be desirable to give administrative assistance for the purpose of ascertaining facts in relation to which the rules of the convention are to be applied. Moreover, in view of the increasing internationalisation of economic relations, the Contracting States have a growing interest in the reciprocal supply of information on the basis of which domestic taxation laws have to be administered, even if there is no question of the application of any particular article of the Convention.

2. Therefore the present Article embodies the rules under which information may be exchanged to the widest possible extent, with a view to laying the proper basis for the implementation of the domestic tax laws of the Contracting States and for the application of specific provisions of the Convention. The text of the Article makes it clear that the exchange of information is not restricted by Articles 1 and 2, so that the information may include particulars about non-residents and may relate to the administration or enforcement of taxes not referred to in Article 2.

3. The matter of administrative assistance for the purpose of tax collection is dealt with in Article 27.

4. In 2002, the Committee on Fiscal Affairs undertook a comprehensive review of Article 26 to ensure that it reflects current country practices. That review also took into account recent developments such as the Model Agreement on Exchange of Information on Tax Matters developed by the OECD Global Forum Working Group on Effective Exchange of Information and the ideal standard of access to bank information as described in the report Improving Access to Bank Information for Tax Purposes. As a result, several changes to both the text of the Article and the Commentary were made in 2005.

4.1 Many of the changes that were then made to the Article were not intended to alter its substance, but instead were made to remove doubts as to its proper interpretation. For instance, the change from "necessary" to "foreseeably relevant" and the insertion of the words "to the administration or enforcement" in paragraph 1 were made to achieve consistency with the Model Agreement on Exchange of Information on Tax Matters and were not intended to alter the effect of the provision. New paragraph 4 was added to incorporate into the text of the Article the general understanding previously expressed in the Commentary (cf. paragraph 19.6). New paragraph 5 was added to reflect current practices among the vast majority of OECD member countries (cf. paragraph 19.10). The insertion of the words "or the oversight of the above" into new paragraph 2, on the other hand, constitutes a reversal of the previous rule.

4.2 The Commentary also has been expanded considerably. This expansion in part reflects the addition of new paragraphs 4 and 5 to the Article. Other changes were made to the Commentary to take into account recent developments and current country practices and more generally to remove doubts as to the proper interpretation of the Article.

II. Commentary on the provisions of the Article

Paragraph 1

5. The main rule concerning the exchange of information is contained in the first sentence of the paragraph. The competent authorities of the Contracting States shall exchange such information as is foreseeably relevant to secure the correct application of the provisions of the Convention or of the domestic laws of the Contracting States concerning taxes of every kind and description imposed in these States even if, in the latter case, a particular Article of the Convention need not be applied. The standard of "foreseeable relevance" is intended to provide for exchange of information in tax matters to the widest possible extent and, at the same time, to clarify that Contracting States are not at liberty to engage in "fishing expeditions" or to request information that is unlikely to be relevant to the tax affairs of a given taxpayer. Contracting States may agree to an alternative formulation of this standard that is consistent with the scope of the Article (e.g. by replacing, "foreseeably relevant" with "necessary" or "relevant"). The scope of

exchange of information covers all tax matters without prejudice to the general rules and legal provisions governing the rights of defendants and witnesses in judicial proceedings. Exchange of information for criminal tax matters can also be based on bilateral or multilateral treaties on mutual legal assistance (to the extent they also apply to tax crimes). In order to keep the exchange of information within the framework of the Convention, a limitation to the exchange of information is set so that information should be given only insofar as the taxation under the domestic taxation laws concerned is not contrary to the Convention.

5.1 The information covered by paragraph 1 is not limited to taxpayer-specific information. The competent authorities may also exchange other sensitive information related to tax administration and compliance improvement, for example risk analysis techniques or tax avoidance or evasion schemes.

5.2 The possibilities of assistance provided by the Article do not limit, nor are they limited by, those contained in existing international agreements or other arrangements between the Contracting States which relate to co-operation in tax matters. Since the exchange of information concerning the application of custom duties has a legal basis in other international instruments, the provisions of these more specialised instruments will generally prevail and the exchange of information concerning custom duties will not, in practice, be governed by the Article.

6. The following examples may clarify the principle dealt with in paragraph 5 above. In all such cases information can be exchanged under paragraph 1.

7. Application of the Convention

a) When applying Article 12, State A where the beneficiary is resident asks State B where the payer is resident, for information concerning the amount of royalty transmitted.

b) Conversely, in order to grant the exemption provided for in Article 12, State B asks State A whether the recipient of the amounts paid is in fact a resident of the last-mentioned State and the beneficial owner of the royalties.

c) Similarly, information may be needed with a view to the proper allocation of taxable profits between associated companies in different States or the adjustment of the profits shown in the accounts of a permanent establishment in one State and in the accounts of the head office in the other State (Articles 7, 9, 23 A and 23 B).

d) Information may be needed for the purposes of applying Article 25.

e) When applying Articles 15 and 23 A, State A, where the employee is resident, informs State B, where the employment is exercised for more than 183 days, of the amount exempted from taxation in State A.

8. Implementation of the domestic laws

a) A company in State A supplies goods to an independent company in State B. State A wishes to know from State B what price the company in State B paid for the goods with a view to a correct application of the provisions of its domestic laws.

b) A company in State A sells goods through a company in State C (possibly a low-tax country) to a company in State B. The companies may or may not be associated. There is no convention between State A and State C, nor between State B and State C. Under the convention between A and B, State A, with a view to ensuring the correct application of the provisions of its domestic laws to the profits made by the company situated in its territory, asks State B what price the company in State B paid for the goods.

c) State A, for the purpose of taxing a company situated in its territory, asks State B, under the convention between A and B, for information about the prices charged by a company in State B, or a group of companies in State B with which the company in State A has no business contacts in order to enable it to check the prices charged by the company in State A by direct comparison (e.g. prices charged by a company or a group of companies in a dominant position). It should be borne in mind that the exchange of information in this case might be a difficult and delicate matter owing in particular to the provisions of subparagraph c) of paragraph 3 relating to business and other secrets.

d) State A, for the purpose of verifying VAT input tax credits claimed by a company situated in its territory for services performed by a company resident in State B, requests confirmation that the cost of services was properly entered into the books and records of the company in State B.

9. The rule laid down in paragraph 1 allows information to be exchanged in three different ways:

a) on request, with a special case in mind, it being understood that the regular sources of information available under the internal taxation procedure should be relied upon in the first place before a request for information is made to the other State;

b) automatically, for example when information about one or various categories of income having their source in one Contracting State and received in the other Contracting State is transmitted systematically to the other State (cf. the OECD Council Recommendation C(81)39, dated 5 May 1981, entitled Recommendation of the Council concerning a standardised form for automatic exchanges of information under international tax agreements, the OECD Council Recommendation C(92)50, dated 23 July 1992, entitled Recommendation of the Council concerning a standard magnetic format for automatic exchange of tax information, the OECD Council Recommendation on the use of Tax Identification Numbers in an international context C(97)29/FINAL dated 13 March 1997, the OECD Council Recommendation C(97)30/FINAL dated 10 July 1997 entitled Recommendation of the Council of the OECD on the Use of the Revised Standard Magnetic Format for Automatic Exchange of Information and the OECD Council Recommendation on the use of the OECD Model Memorandum of Understanding on Automatic Exchange of Information for Tax Purposes C(2001)28/FINAL);

c) spontaneously, for example in the case of a State having acquired through certain investigations, information which it supposes to be of interest to the other State.

9.1 These three forms of exchange (on request, automatic and spontaneous) may also be combined. It should also be stressed that the Article does not restrict the possibilities of exchanging information to these methods and that the Contracting States may use other techniques to obtain information which may be relevant to both Contracting States such as simultaneous examinations, tax examinations abroad and industry-wide exchange of information. These techniques are fully described in the publication Tax Information Exchange between OECD Member Countries: A Survey of Current Practices and can be summarised as follows:

— a simultaneous examination is an arrangement between two or more parties to examine simultaneously each in its own territory, the tax affairs of (a) taxpayer(s) in which they have a common or related interest, with a view of exchanging any relevant information which they so obtain (see the OECD Council

Recommendation C(92)81, dated 23 July 1992, on an OECD Model agreement for the undertaking of simultaneous examinations);

— a tax examination abroad allows for the possibility to obtain information through the presence of representatives of the competent authority of the requesting Contracting State. To the extent allowed by its domestic law, a Contracting State may permit authorised representatives of the other Contracting State to enter the first Contracting State to interview individuals or examine a person's books and records, – or to be present at such interviews or examinations carried out by the tax authorities of the first Contracting State – in accordance with procedures mutually agreed upon by the competent authorities. Such a request might arise, for example, where the taxpayer in a Contracting State is permitted to keep records in the other Contracting State. This type of assistance is granted on a reciprocal basis. Countries' laws and practices differ as to the scope of rights granted to foreign tax officials. For instance, there are States where a foreign tax official will be prevented from any active participation in an investigation or examination on the territory of a country; there are also States where such participation is only possible with the taxpayer's consent. The Joint Council of Europe/OECD Convention on Mutual Administrative Assistance in Tax Matters specifically addresses tax examinations abroad in its Article 9;

— an industry-wide exchange of information is the exchange of tax information especially concerning a whole economic sector (e.g. the oil or pharmaceutical industry, the banking sector, etc.) and not taxpayers in particular.

10. The manner in which the exchange of information agreed to in the Convention will finally be effected can be decided upon by the competent authorities of the Contracting States. For example, Contracting States may wish to use electronic or other communication and information technologies, including appropriate security systems, to improve the timeliness and quality of exchanges of information. Contracting States which are required, according to their law, to observe data protection laws, may wish to include provisions in their bilateral conventions concerning the protection of personal data exchanged. Data protection concerns the rights and fundamental freedoms of an individual, and in particular, the right to privacy, with regard to automatic processing of personal data. See, for example, the Council of Europe Convention for the Protection of Individuals with regard to Automatic Processing of Personal Data of 28 January 1981.

10.1 Before 2000, the paragraph only authorised the exchange of information, and the use of the information exchanged, in relation to the taxes covered by the Convention under the general rules of Article 2. As drafted, the paragraph did not oblige the requested State to comply with a request for information concerning the imposition of a sales tax as such a tax was not covered by the Convention. The paragraph was then amended so as to apply to the exchange of information concerning any tax imposed on behalf of the Contracting States, or of their political subdivisions or local authorities, and to allow the use of the information exchanged for purposes of the application of all such taxes. Some Contracting States may not, however, be in a position to exchange information, or to use the information obtained from a treaty partner, in relation to taxes that are not covered by the Convention under the general rules of Article 2. Such States are free to restrict the scope of paragraph 1 of the Article to the taxes covered by the Convention.

10.2 In some cases, a Contracting State may need to receive information in a particular form to satisfy its evidentiary or other legal requirements. Such forms may include depositions of witnesses and authenticated copies of original records. Contracting States should endeavour as far as possible to accommodate such requests. Under paragraph 3, the requested State may decline to provide the information in the specific form requested if, for instance, the requested form is not known or permitted under its law or administrative practice. A refusal to provide the information in the form requested does not affect the obligation to provide the information.

10.3 Nothing in the Convention prevents the application of the provisions of the Article to the exchange of information that existed prior to the entry into force of the Convention, as long as the assistance with respect to this information is provided after the Convention has entered into force and the provisions of the Article have become effective. Contracting States may find it useful, however, to clarify the extent to which the provisions of the Article are applicable to such information, in particular when the provisions of that convention will have effect with respect to taxes arising or levied from a certain time.

Paragraph 2

11. Reciprocal assistance between tax administrations is feasible only if each administration is assured that the other administration will treat with proper confidence the information which it will receive in the course of their co-operation. The confidentiality rules of paragraph 2 apply to all types of information received under paragraph 1, including both information provided in a request and information transmitted in response to a request. The maintenance of secrecy in the receiving Contracting State is a matter of domestic laws. It is therefore provided in paragraph 2 that information communicated under the provisions of the Convention shall be treated as secret in the receiving State in the same manner as information obtained under the domestic laws of that State. Sanctions for the violation of such secrecy in that State will be governed by the administrative and penal laws of that State.

11.1 (Renumbered on 15 July 2005)

11.2 (Renumbered on 15 July 2005)

12. The information obtained may be disclosed only to persons and authorities involved in the assessment or collection of, the enforcement or prosecution in respect of, the determination of appeals in relation to the taxes with respect to which information may be exchanged according to the first sentence of paragraph 1, or the oversight of the above. This means that the information may also be communicated to the taxpayer, his proxy or to the witnesses. This also means that information can be disclosed to governmental or judicial authorities charged with deciding whether such information should be released to the taxpayer, his proxy or to the witnesses. The information received by a Contracting State may be used by such persons or authorities

only for the purposes mentioned in paragraph 2. Furthermore, information covered by paragraph 1, whether taxpayer-specific or not, should not be disclosed to persons or authorities not mentioned in paragraph 2, regardless of domestic information disclosure laws such as freedom of information or other legislation that allows greater access to governmental documents.

12.1 Information can also be disclosed to oversight bodies. Such oversight bodies include authorities that supervise tax administration and enforcement authorities as part of the general administration of the Government of a Contracting State. In their bilateral negotiations, however, Contracting States may depart from this principle and agree to exclude the disclosure of information to such supervisory bodies.

12.2 The information received by a Contracting State may not be disclosed to a third country unless there is an express provision in the bilateral treaty between the Contracting States allowing such disclosure.

12.3 Similarly, if the information appears to be of value to the receiving State for other purposes than those referred to in paragraph 12, that State may not use the information for such other purposes but it must resort to means specifically designed for those purposes (e.g. in case of a non-fiscal crime, to a treaty concerning judicial assistance). However, Contracting States may wish to allow the sharing of tax information by tax authorities with other law enforcement agencies and judicial authorities on certain high priority matters (e.g., to combat money laundering, corruption, terrorism financing). Contracting States wishing to broaden the purposes for which they may use information exchanged under this Article may do so by adding the following text to the end of paragraph 2:
"Notwithstanding the foregoing, information received by a Contracting State may be used for other purposes when such information may be used for such other purposes under the laws of both States and the competent authority of the supplying State authorises such use."

13. As stated in paragraph 12, the information obtained can be communicated to the persons and authorities mentioned and on the basis of the last sentence of paragraph 2 of the Article can be disclosed by them in court sessions held in public or in decisions which reveal the name of the taxpayer. Once information is used in public

court proceedings or in court decisions and thus rendered public, it is clear that from that moment such information can be quoted from the court files or decisions for other purposes even as possible evidence. But this does not mean that the persons and authorities mentioned in paragraph 2 are allowed to provide on request additional information received. If either or both of the Contracting States object to the information being made public by courts in this way, or, once the information has been made public in this way, to the information being used for other purposes, because this is not the normal procedure under their domestic laws, they should state this expressly in their convention.

Paragraph 3

14. This paragraph contains certain limitations to the main rule in favour of the requested State. In the first place, the paragraph contains the clarification that a Contracting State is not bound to go beyond its own internal laws and administrative practice in putting information at the disposal of the other Contracting State. However, internal provisions concerning tax secrecy should not be interpreted as constituting an obstacle to the exchange of information under the present Article. As mentioned above, the authorities of the requesting State are obliged to observe secrecy with regard to information received under this Article.

14.1 Some countries' laws include procedures for notifying the person who provided the information and/or the taxpayer that is subject to the enquiry prior to the supply of information. Such notification procedures may be an important aspect of the rights provided under domestic law. They can help prevent mistakes (e.g. in cases of mistaken identity) and facilitate exchange (by allowing taxpayers who are notified to co-operate voluntarily with the tax authorities in the requesting State). Notification procedures should not, however, be applied in a manner that, in the particular circumstances of the request, would frustrate the efforts of the requesting State. In other words, they should not prevent or unduly delay effective exchange of information. For instance, notification procedures should permit exceptions from prior notification, e.g. in cases in which the information request is of a very urgent nature or the notification is likely to undermine the chance of success of the investigation conducted by the requesting State. A Contracting State that under its domestic law is required to notify the person who provided the information and/or the taxpayer that an exchange of information is proposed should inform its treaty partners in writing that it has this requirement and what the consequences are for its obligations in relation to mutual assistance. Such information should be provided to the other Contracting State when a convention is concluded and thereafter whenever the relevant rules are modified.

15. Furthermore, the requested State does not need to go so far as to carry out administrative measures that are not permitted under the laws or practice of the requesting State or to supply items of information that are not obtainable under the laws or in the normal course of administration of the requesting State. It follows

that a Contracting State cannot take advantage of the information system of the other Contracting State if it is wider than its own system. Thus, a State may refuse to provide information where the requesting State would be precluded by law from obtaining or providing the information or where the requesting State's administrative practices (e.g., failure to provide sufficient administrative resources) result in a lack of reciprocity. However, it is recognised that too rigorous an application of the principle of reciprocity could frustrate effective exchange of information and that reciprocity should be interpreted in a broad and pragmatic manner. Different countries will necessarily have different mechanisms for obtaining and providing information. Variations in practices and procedures should not be used as a basis for denying a request unless the effect of these variations would be to limit in a significant way the requesting State's overall ability to obtain and provide the information if the requesting State itself received a legitimate request from the requested State.

15.1 The principle of reciprocity has no application where the legal system or administrative practice of only one country provides for a specific procedure. For instance, a country requested to provide information could not point to the absence of a ruling regime in the country requesting information and decline to provide information on a ruling it has granted, based on a reciprocity argument. Of course, where the requested information itself is not obtainable under the laws or in the normal course of the administrative practice of the requesting State, a requested State may decline such a request.

15.2 Most countries recognise under their domestic laws that information cannot be obtained from a person to the extent that such person can claim the privilege against self-incrimination. A requested State may, therefore, decline to provide information if the requesting State would have been precluded by its own self-incrimination rules from obtaining the information under similar circumstances. In practice, however, the privilege against self-incrimination should have little, if any, application in connection with most information requests. The privilege against self-incrimination is personal and cannot be claimed by an individual who himself is not at risk of criminal prosecution. The overwhelming majority of information requests seek to obtain information from third parties such as banks, intermediaries or the other party to a contract and not from the individual under investigation. Furthermore, the privilege against self-incrimination generally does not attach to persons other than natural persons.

16. Information is deemed to be obtainable in the normal course of administration if it is in the possession of the tax authorities or can be obtained by them in the normal procedure of tax determination, which may include special investigations or special examination of the business accounts kept by the taxpayer or other persons, provided that the tax authorities would make similar investigations or examinations for their own purposes.

17. The requested State is at liberty to refuse to give information in the cases referred to in the paragraphs above. However if it does give the requested information, it remains within the framework of the agreement on the exchange of information which is laid down in the Convention; consequently it cannot be objected that this State has failed to observe the obligation to secrecy.

18. If the structure of the information systems of two Contracting States is very different, the conditions under subparagraphs a) and b) of paragraph 3 will lead to the result that the Contracting States exchange very little information or perhaps none at all. In such a case, the Contracting States may find it appropriate to broaden the scope of the exchange of information.

18.1 Unless otherwise agreed to by the Contracting States, it can be assumed that the requested information could be obtained by the requesting State in a similar situation if that State has not indicated to the contrary.

19. In addition to the limitations referred to above, subparagraph c) of paragraph 3 contains a reservation concerning the disclosure of certain secret information. Secrets mentioned in this subparagraph should not be taken in too wide a sense. Before invoking this provision, a Contracting State should carefully weigh if the interests of the taxpayer really justify its application. Otherwise it is clear that too wide an interpretation would in many cases render ineffective the exchange of information provided for in the Convention. The observations made in paragraph 17 above apply here as well. The requested State in protecting the interests of its taxpayers is given a certain discretion to refuse the requested information, but if it does supply the information deliberately the taxpayer cannot allege an infraction of the rules of secrecy.

19.1 In its deliberations regarding the application of secrecy rules, the Contracting State should also take into account the confidentiality rules of paragraph 2 of the Article. The domestic laws and practices of the requesting State together with the obligations imposed under paragraph 2, may ensure that the information cannot be used for the types of unauthorised purposes against which the trade or other secrecy rules are intended to protect. Thus, a Contracting State may decide to supply the information where it finds that there is no reasonable basis for assuming that a taxpayer involved may suffer any adverse consequences incompatible with information exchange.

19.2 In most cases of information exchange no issue of trade, business or other secret will arise. A trade or business secret is generally understood to mean facts and circumstances that are of considerable economic importance and that can be exploited practically and the unauthorised use of which may lead to serious damage (e.g. may lead to severe financial hardship). The determination, assessment or collection of taxes as such could not be considered to result in serious damage. Financial information, including books and records, does not by its nature constitute a trade, business or other secret. In certain limited cases, however, the disclosure of financial information might reveal a trade, business or other secret. For instance, a request for information on certain purchase records may raise such an issue if the disclosure of such information revealed the proprietary formula used in the manufacture of a product. The protection of such information may also extend to information in the possession of third persons. For instance, a bank might hold a pending patent application for safe keeping or a secret trade process or formula might be described in a loan application or in a contract held by a bank. In such circumstances, details of the trade, business or other secret should be excised from the documents and the remaining financial information exchanged accordingly.

19.3 A requested State may decline to disclose information relating to confidential communications between attorneys, solicitors or other admitted legal representatives in their role as such and their clients to the extent that the communications are protected from disclosure under domestic law. However, the scope of protection afforded to such confidential communications should be narrowly defined. Such protection does not attach to documents or records delivered to an attorney, solicitor or other admitted legal representative in an attempt to protect such documents or records from disclosure required by law. Also, information on the identity of a person such as a director or beneficial owner of a company is typically not protected as a confidential communication. Whilst the scope of protection afforded to confidential communications might differ among states, it should not be overly broad so as to hamper effective exchange of information. Communications between attorneys, solicitors or other admitted legal representatives and their clients are only confidential if, and to the extent that, such representatives act in their capacity as attorneys, solicitors or other admitted legal representatives and not in a different capacity, such as nominee shareholders, trustees, settlors, company directors or under a power of attorney to represent a company in its business affairs. An assertion that information is protected as a confidential communication between an attorney, solicitor or other admitted legal representative and its client should be adjudicated exclusively in the Contracting State under the laws of which it arises. Thus, it is not intended that the courts of the requested State should adjudicate claims based on the laws of the requesting State.

19.4 Contracting States wishing to refer expressly to the protection afforded to confidential communications between a client and an attorney, solicitor or other admitted legal representative may do so by adding the following text at the end of paragraph 3:

"d)

to obtain or provide information which would reveal confidential communications between a client and an attorney, solicitor or other admitted legal representative where such communications are:

(i) produced for the purposes of seeking or providing legal advice or

(ii) produced for the purposes of use in existing or contemplated legal proceedings."

19.5 Paragraph 3 also includes a limitation with regard to information which concerns the vital interests of the State itself. To this end, it is stipulated that Contracting States do not have to supply information the disclosure of which would be contrary to public policy (ordre public). However, this limitation should only become relevant in extreme cases. For instance, such a case could arise if a tax investigation in the requesting State were motivated by political, racial, or religious persecution. The limitation may also be invoked where the information constitutes a state secret, for instance sensitive information held by secret services the disclosure of which would be contrary to the vital interests of the requested State. Thus, issues of public policy (ordre public) rarely arise in the context of information exchange between treaty partners.

Paragraph 4

19.6 Paragraph 4 was added in 2005 to deal explicitly with the obligation to exchange information in situations where the requested information is not needed by the requested State for domestic tax purposes. Prior to the addition of paragraph 4 this obligation was not expressly stated in the Article, but was clearly evidenced by the practices followed by member countries which showed that, when collecting information requested by a treaty partner, Contracting States often use the special examining or investigative powers provided by their laws for purposes of levying their domestic taxes even though they do not themselves need the information for these purposes. This principle is also stated in the report Improving Access to Bank Information for Tax Purposes.

19.7 According to paragraph 4, Contracting States must use their information gathering measures, even though invoked solely to provide information to the other Contracting State. The term "information gathering measures" means laws and administrative or judicial procedures that enable a Contracting State to obtain and provide the requested information.

19.8 The second sentence of paragraph 4 makes clear that the obligation contained in paragraph 4 is subject to the limitations of paragraph 3 but also provides that such limitations cannot be construed to form the basis for declining to supply information where a country's laws or purposes, it may, for instance, decline to supply the information to the extent that the provision of the information would disclose a trade secret.

19.9 For many countries the combination of paragraph 4 and their domestic law provide a sufficient basis for using their information gathering measures to obtain the requested information even in the absence of a domestic tax interest in the information. Other countries, however, may wish to clarify expressly in the convention that Contracting States must ensure that their competent authorities have the necessary powers to do so. Contracting States wishing to clarify this point may replace paragraph 4 with the following text:

4. In order to effectuate the exchange of information as provided in paragraph 1, each Contracting State shall take the necessary measures, including legislation, rule-making, or administrative arrangements, to ensure that its compe¬tent authority has sufficient powers under its domestic law to obtain information for the exchange of information regardless of whether that Contracting State may need such information for its own tax purposes."

Paragraph 5

19.10 Paragraph 1 imposes a positive obligation on a Contracting State to exchange all types of information. Paragraph 5 is intended to ensure that the limitations of paragraph 3 cannot be used to prevent the exchange of information held by banks, other financial institutions, nominees, agents and fiduciaries as well as ownership information. Whilst paragraph 5, which was added in 2005, represents a change in the structure of the Article it should not be interpreted as suggesting that the previous version of the Article did not authorise the exchange of such information. The vast majority of OECD member countries already exchanged such information under the previous version of the Article and the addition of paragraph 5 merely reflects current practice.

19.11 Paragraph 5 stipulates that a Contracting State shall not decline to supply information to a treaty partner solely because the information is held by a bank or other financial institution. Thus, paragraph 5 overrides paragraph 3 to the extent that paragraph 3 would otherwise permit a requested Contracting State to decline to supply information on grounds of bank secrecy. The addition of this paragraph to the Article reflects the international trend in this area as reflected in the Model Agreement on Exchange of Information on Tax Matters and as described in the report, Improving Access to Bank Information for Tax Purposes. In accordance with that report, access to information held by banks or other financial institutions may be by direct means or indirectly through a judicial or administrative process. The procedure for indirect access should not be so burdensome and time-consuming as to act as an impediment to access to bank information.

19.12 Paragraph 5 also provides that a Contracting State shall not decline to supply information solely because the information is held by persons acting in an agency or fiduciary capacity. For instance, if a Contracting State had a law under which all information held by a fiduciary was treated as a "professional secret" merely because it was held by a fiduciary, such State could not use such law as a basis for declining to provide the information to the other Contracting State. A person is generally said to act in a "fiduciary capacity" when the business which the person transacts, or the money or property which the person handles, is not its own or for its own benefit, but for the benefit of another person as to whom the fiduciary stands in a relation implying and necessitating confidence and trust on the one part and good faith on the other part, such as a trustee. The term "agency" is very broad and includes all forms of corporate service providers (e.g. company formation agents, trust companies, registered agents, lawyers).

19.13 Finally, paragraph 5 states that a Contracting State shall not decline to supply information solely because it relates to an ownership interest in a person, including companies and partnerships, foundations or similar organisational structures. Information requests cannot be declined merely because domestic laws or practices may treat ownership information as a trade or other secret.

19.14 Paragraph 5 does not preclude a Contracting State from invoking paragraph 3 to refuse to supply information held by a bank, financial institution, a person acting in an agency or fiduciary capacity or information relating to ownership interests. However, such refusal must be based on reasons u nrelated to the person's status as a bank, financial institution, agent, fiduciary or nominee, or the fact that the information relates to ownership interests. For instance, a legal representative acting for a client may be acting in an agency capacity but for any information protected as a confidential communication between attorneys, solicitors or other admitted legal representatives and their clients, paragraph 3 continues to provide a possible basis for declining to supply the information.

19.15 The following examples illustrate the application of paragraph 5:

a) Company X owns a majority of the stock in a subsidiary company Y, and both companies are incorporated under the laws of State A. State B is conducting a tax examination of business operations of company Y in State B. In the course of this examination the question of both direct and indirect ownership in company Y becomes relevant and State B makes a request to State A for ownership information of any person in company Y's chain of ownership. In its reply State A should provide to State B ownership information for both company X and Y.

b) An individual subject to tax in State A maintains a bank account with Bank B in State B. State A is examining the income tax return of the individual and makes a request to State B for all bank account income and asset information held by Bank B in order to determine whether there were deposits of untaxed earned income. State B should provide the requested bank information to State A.

Observations on the Commentary

20. Japan wishes to indicate that with respect to paragraph 11 above, it would be difficult for Japan, in view of its strict domestic laws and administrative practice as to the procedure to make public the information obtained under the domestic laws, to provide information requested unless a requesting State has comparable domestic laws and administrative practice as to this procedure.

21. In connection with paragraph 15.1. Greece wishes to clarify that according to Article 28 of the Greek Constitution international tax treaties are applied under the terms of reciprocity.

22. (Deleted on 15 July 2005)
Reservations on the Article

23. Austria reserves the right not to include paragraph 5 in its conventions. However, Austria is authorised to exchange information held by a bank or other financial institution where such information is requested within the framework of a criminal investigation which is carried on in the requesting State concerning the commitment of tax fraud.

24. Switzerland reserves its position on paragraphs 1 and 5. It will propose to limit the scope of this Article to information necessary for carrying out the provisions of the Convention. This reservation shall not apply in cases involving acts of fraud subject to imprisonment according to the laws of both Contracting States.

25. Luxembourg reserves the right not to include paragraph 5 in its conventions.

26. Belgium reserves the right not to include paragraph 5 in its conventions. Where paragraph 5 is included in one of its conventions, the exchange of information held by a bank or other financial institution is restricted to the exchange on request of information concerning both a specific taxpayer and a specific financial institution.

The 2002 Model Agreement on Exchange of Information on Tax Matters and its Commentary

I. INTRODUCTION

1. The purpose of this Agreement is to promote international co-operation in tax matters through exchange of information.

2. The Agreement was developed by the OECD Global Forum Working Group on Effective Exchange of Information ("the Working Group"). The Working Group consisted of representatives from OECD Member countries as well as delegates from Aruba, Bermuda, Bahrain, Cayman Islands, Cyprus, Isle of Man, Malta, Mauritius, the Netherlands Antilles, the Seychelles and San Marino.

3. The Agreement grew out of the work undertaken by the OECD to address harmful tax practices. See the 1998 OECD Report "*Harmful Tax Competition: An Emerging Global Issue*" (the "1998 Report"). The 1998 Report identified "the lack of effective exchange of information" as one of the key criteria in determining harmful tax practices. The mandate of the Working Group was to develop a legal instrument that could be used to establish effective exchange of information. The Agreement represents the standard of effective exchange of information for the purposes of the OECD's initiative on harmful tax practices.

4. This Agreement is not a binding instrument but contains two models for bilateral agreements drawn up in the light of the commitments undertaken by the OECD and the committed jurisdictions. In this context, it is important that financial centres throughout the world meet the standards of tax information exchange set out in this document. As many economies as possible should be encouraged to co-operate in this important endeavour. It is not in the interest of participating economies that the implementation of the standard contained in the Agreement should lead to the migration of business to economies that do not co-operate in the exchange of information. To avoid

this result requires measures to defend the integrity of tax systems against the impact of a lack of co-operation in tax information exchange matters. The OECD members and committed jurisdictions have to engage in an ongoing dialogue to work towards implementation of the standard. An adequate framework will be jointly established by the OECD and the committed jurisdictions for this purpose particularly since such a framework would help to achieve a level playing field where no party is unfairly disadvantaged.

5. The Agreement is presented as both a multilateral instrument and a model for bilateral treaties or agreements. The multilateral instrument is not a "multilateral" agreement in the traditional sense. Instead, it provides the basis for an integrated bundle of bilateral treaties. A Party to the multilateral Agreement would only be bound by the Agreement vis- à-vis the specific parties with which it agrees to be bound. Thus, a party wishing to be bound by the multilateral Agreement must specify in its instrument of ratification, approval or acceptance the party or parties vis-à-vis which it wishes to be so bound. The Agreement then enters into force, and creates rights and obligations, only as between those parties that have mutually identified each other in their instruments of ratification, approval or acceptance that have been deposited with the depositary of the Agreement. The bilateral version is intended to serve as a model for bilateral exchange of information agreements. As such, modifications to the text may be agreed in bilateral agreements to implement the standard set in the model.

6. As mentioned above, the Agreement is intended to establish the standard of what constitutes effective exchange of information for the purposes of the OECD's initiative on harmful tax practices. However, the purpose of the Agreement is not to prescribe a specific format for how this standard should be achieved. Thus, the Agreement in either of its forms is only one of several ways in which the standard can be implemented. Other instruments, including double taxation agreements, may also be used provided both parties agree to do so, given that other instruments are usually wider in scope.

7. For each Article in the Agreement there is a detailed commentary intended to illustrate or interpret its provisions. The relevance of the Commentary for the interpretation of the Agreement is determined by principles of international law. In the bilateral context, parties wishing to ensure that the Commentary is an authoritative interpretation might insert a specific reference to the Commentary in the text of the exchange instrument, for instance in the provision equivalent to Article 4, paragraph 2.

II. TEXT OF THE AGREEMENT

MULTILATERAL VERSION

The Parties to this Agreement, desiring to facilitate the exchange of information with respect to taxes have agreed as follows:

BILATERAL VERSION

The government of _______ and the government of ______, desiring to facilitate the exchange of information with respect to taxes have agreed as follows:

Article 1

Object and Scope of the Agreement

The competent authorities of the Contracting Parties shall provide assistance through exchange of information that is foreseeably relevant to the administration and enforcement of the domestic laws of the Contracting Parties concerning taxes covered by this Agreement. Such information shall include information that is foreseeably relevant to the determination, assessment and collection of such taxes, the recovery and enforcement of tax claims, or the investigation or prosecution of tax matters. Information shall be exchanged in accordance with the provisions of this Agreement and shall be treated as confidential in the manner provided in Article 8. The rights and safeguards secured to persons by the laws or administrative practice of the requested Party remain applicable to the extent that they do not unduly prevent or delay effective exchange of information.

Article 2

Jurisdiction

A Requested Party is not obligated to provide information which is neither held by its authorities nor in the possession or control of persons who are within its territorial jurisdiction.

Article 3

Taxes Covered

MULTILATERAL VERSION

1. This Agreement shall apply:

a) to the following taxes imposed by or on behalf of a Contracting Party:

i) taxes on income or profits;

ii) taxes on capital;

iii) taxes on net wealth;

iv) estate, inheritance or gift taxes;

b) to the taxes in categories referred to in subparagraph a) above, which are imposed by or on behalf of political sub-divisions or local authorities of the Contracting Parties if listed in the instrument of ratification, acceptance or approval.

2. The Contracting Parties, in their instruments of ratification, acceptance or approval, may agree that the Agreement shall also apply to indirect taxes.

3. This Agreement shall also apply to any identical taxes imposed after the date of entry into force of the Agreement in addition to or in place of the existing taxes. This Agreement shall

BILATERAL VERSION

1. The taxes which are the subject of this Agreement are:

a) in country A, ____________________;

b) in country B, ____________________

2. This Agreement shall also apply to any identical taxes imposed after the date of signature of the Agreement in addition to or in place of the existing taxes. This Agreement shall also apply to any substantially similar taxes imposed after the date of signature of the Agreement in addition to or in place of the existing taxes if the competent authorities of the Contracting Parties so agree. Furthermore, the taxes covered may be expanded or modified by mutual agreement of the Contracting Parties in the form of an exchange of letters. The competent authorities of the Contracting Parties shall notify each other of any substantial changes to the taxation and related information gathering measures covered by the Agreement.

also apply to any substantially similar taxes imposed after the date of entry into force of the Agreement in addition to or in place of the existing taxes if the competent authorities of the Contracting Parties so agree. Furthermore, the taxes covered may be expanded or modified by mutual agreement of the Contracting Parties in the form of an exchange of letters. The competent authorities of the Contracting Parties shall notify each other of any substantial changes to the taxation and related information gathering measures covered by the Agreement.

Article 4

Definitions

MULTILATERAL VERSION	BILATERAL VERSION
1. For the purposes of this Agreement, unless otherwise defined:	
a) the term "Contracting Party" means any party that has deposited an instrument of ratification, acceptance or approval with the depositary;	a) the term "Contracting Party" means country A or country B as the context requires;
b) the term "competent authority" means the authorities designated by a Contracting Party in its instrument of acceptance, ratification or approval;	b) the term "competent authority" means i) in the case of Country A, ________________; ii) in the case of Country B, ________________;

c) the term "person" includes an individual, a company and any other body of persons;

d) the term "company" means any body corporate or any entity that is treated as a body corporate for tax purposes;

e) the term "publicly traded company" means any company whose principal class of shares is listed on a recognised stock exchange provided its listed shares can be readily purchased or sold by the public. Shares can be purchased or sold "by the public" if the purchase or sale of shares is not implicitly or explicitly restricted to a limited group of investors;

f) the term "principal class of shares" means the class or classes of shares representing a majority of the voting power and value of the company;

g) the term "recognised stock exchange" means any stock exchange agreed upon by the competent authorities of the Contracting Parties;

h) the term "collective investment fund or scheme" means any pooled investment vehicle, irrespective of legal form. The term "public collective investment fund or scheme" means any collective investment fund or scheme provided the units, shares or other interests in the fund or scheme can be readily purchased, sold or redeemed by the public. Units, shares or other interests in the fund or scheme can be readily purchased, sold or redeemed "by the public" if the purchase, sale or redemption is not implicitly or explicitly restricted to a limited group of investors;

i) the term "tax" means any tax to which the Agreement applies;

j) the term "applicant Party" means the Contracting Party requesting information;

k) the term "requested Party" means the Contracting Party requested to provide information;

l) the term "information gathering measures" means laws and administrative or judicial procedures that enable a Contracting Party to obtain and provide the requested information;

m) the term "information" means any fact, statement or record in any form whatever;

n) the term "depositary" means the Secretary-General of the Organisation for Economic Co-operation and Development;	*This paragraph would not be necessary*

o) the term "criminal tax matters" means tax matters involving intentional conduct which is liable to prosecution under the criminal laws of the applicant Party;

p) the term " criminal laws" means all criminal laws designated as such under domestic law irrespective of whether contained in the tax laws, the criminal code or other statutes.

2. As regards the application of this Agreement at any time by a Contracting Party, any term not defined therein shall, unless the context otherwise requires, have the meaning that it has at that time under the law of that Party, any meaning under the applicable tax laws of that Party prevailing over a meaning given to the term under other laws of that Party.

Article 5

Exchange of Information Upon Request

1. The competent authority of the requested Party shall provide upon request information for the purposes referred to in Article 1. Such information shall be exchanged without regard to whether the conduct being investigated would constitute a crime under the

laws of the requested Party if such conduct occurred in the requested Party.

2. If the information in the possession of the competent authority of the requested Party is not sufficient to enable it to comply with the request for information, that Party shall use all relevant information gathering measures to provide the applicant Party with the information requested, notwithstanding that the requested Party may not need such information for its own tax purposes.

3. If specifically requested by the competent authority of an applicant Party, the competent authority of the requested Party shall provide information under this Article, to the extent allowable under its domestic laws, in the form of depositions of witnesses and authenticated copies of original records.

4. Each Contracting Party shall ensure that its competent authorities for the purposes specified in Article 1 of the Agreement, have the authority to obtain and provide upon request:

a) information held by banks, other financial institutions, and any person acting in an agency or fiduciary capacity including nominees and trustees;

b) information regarding the ownership of companies, partnerships, trusts, foundations, "Anstalten" and other persons, including, within the constraints of Article 2, ownership information on all such persons in an ownership chain; in the case of trusts, information on settlors, trustees and beneficiaries; and in the case of foundations, information on founders, members of the foundation council and beneficiaries. Further, this Agreement does not create an obligation on the Contracting Parties to obtain or provide ownership information with respect to publicly traded companies or public collective investment funds or schemes unless such information can be obtained without giving rise to disproportionate difficulties.

5. The competent authority of the applicant Party shall provide the following information to the competent authority of the requested Party when making a request for information under the Agreement to demonstrate the foreseeable relevance of the information to the request:

(a) the identity of the person under examination or investigation;

(b) a statement of the information sought including its nature and the form in which the applicant Party wishes to receive the information from the requested Party;

(c) the tax purpose for which the information is sought;

(d) grounds for believing that the information requested is held in the requested Party or is in the possession or control of a person within the jurisdiction of the requested Party;

(e) to the extent known, the name and address of any person believed to be in possession of the requested information;

(f) a statement that the request is in conformity with the law and administrative practices of the applicant Party, that if the requested information was within the jurisdiction of the applicant Party then the competent authority of the applicant Party would be able to obtain the information under the laws of the applicant Party or in the normal course of administrative practice and that it is in conformity with this Agreement;

(g) a statement that the applicant Party has pursued all means available in its own territory to obtain the information, except those that would give rise to disproportionate difficulties.

6. The competent authority of the requested Party shall forward the requested information as promptly as possible to the applicant Party. To ensure a prompt response, the competent authority of the requested Party shall:

a) Confirm receipt of a request in writing to the competent authority of the applicant Party and shall notify the competent authority of the applicant Party of deficiencies in the request, if any, within 60 days of the receipt of the request.

b) If the competent authority of the requested Party has been unable to obtain and provide the information within 90 days of receipt of the request, including if it encounters obstacles in furnishing the information or it refuses to furnish the information, it shall immediately inform the applicant Party, explaining the reason for its inability, the nature of the obstacles or the reasons for its refusal.

Article 6

Tax Examinations Abroad

MULTILATERAL VERSION

1. A Contracting Party may allow representatives of the competent authority of another Contracting Party to enter the territory of the first-mentioned Party to interview individuals and examine records with the written consent of the persons concerned. The competent authority of the second-mentioned Party shall notify the competent authority of the first-mentioned Party of the time and place of the meeting with the individuals concerned.

2. At the request of the competent authority of a Contracting Party, the competent authority of another Contracting Party may allow representatives of the competent authority of the first-mentioned Party to be present at the appropriate part of a tax examination in the second-mentioned Party.

3. If the request referred to in paragraph 2 is acceded to, the competent authority of the Contracting Party conducting the examination shall, as soon as possible, notify the competent authority of the other Party about the time and place of the examination, the authority or official designated to carry out the examination and the procedures and conditions required by the first-mentioned Party for the conduct of the examination. All decisions with respect to the conduct of the tax examination shall be made by the Party conducting the examination.

BILATERAL VERSION

1. A Contracting Party may allow representatives of the competent authority of the other Contracting Party to enter the territory of the first-mentioned Party to interview individuals and examine records with the written consent of the persons concerned. The competent authority of the second-mentioned Party shall notify the competent authority of the first-mentioned Party of the time and place of the meeting with the individuals concerned.

2. At the request of the competent authority of one Contracting Party, the competent authority of the other Contracting Party may allow representatives of the competent authority of the first-mentioned Party to be present at the appropriate part of a tax examination in the second-mentioned Party.

3. If the request referred to in paragraph 2 is acceded to, the competent authority of the Contracting Party conducting the examination shall, as soon as possible, notify the competent authority of the other Party about the time and place of the examination, the authority or official designated to carry out the examination and the procedures and conditions required by the first-mentioned Party for the conduct of the examination. All decisions with respect to the conduct of the tax examination shall be made by the Party conducting the examination.

Article 7

Possibility of Declining a Request

1. The requested Party shall not be required to obtain or provide information that the applicant Party would not be able to obtain under its own laws for purposes of the administration or enforcement of its own tax laws. The competent authority of the requested Party may decline to assist where the request is not made in conformity with this Agreement.

2. The provisions of this Agreement shall not impose on a Contracting Party the obligation to supply information which would disclose any trade, business, industrial, commercial or professional secret or trade process. Notwithstanding the foregoing, information of the type referred to in Article 5, paragraph 4 shall not be treated as such a secret or trade process merely because it meets the criteria in that paragraph.

3. The provisions of this Agreement shall not impose on a Contracting Party the obligation to obtain or provide information, which would reveal confidential communications between a client and an attorney, solicitor or other admitted legal representative where such communications are:

(a) produced for the purposes of seeking or providing legal advice or

(b) produced for the purposes of use in existing or contemplated legal proceedings.

4. The requested Party may decline a request for information if the disclosure of the information would be contrary to public policy (ordre public).

5. A request for information shall not be refused on the ground that the tax claim giving rise to the request is disputed.

6. The requested Party may decline a request for information if the information is requested by the applicant Party to administer or enforce a provision of the tax law of the applicant Party, or any requirement connected therewith, which discriminates against a national of the requested Party as compared with a national of the applicant Party in the same circumstances.

Article 8

Confidentiality

Any information received by a Contracting Party under this Agreement shall be treated as confidential and may be disclosed only to persons or authorities (including courts and administrative bodies) in the jurisdiction of the Contracting Party concerned with the assessment or collection of, the enforcement or prosecution in respect of, or the determination of appeals in relation to, the taxes covered by this Agreement. Such persons or authorities shall use such information only for such purposes. They may disclose the information in public court proceedings or in judicial decisions. The information may not be disclosed to any other person or entity or authority or any other jurisdiction without the express written consent of the competent authority of the requested Party.

Article 9

Costs

Incidence of costs incurred in providing assistance shall be agreed by the Contracting Parties.

Article 10

Implementation Legislation

The Contracting Parties shall enact any legislation necessary to comply with, and give effect to, the terms of the Agreement.

Article 11

Language

This article may not be required.

Requests for assistance and answers thereto shall be drawn up in English, French or any other language agreed bilaterally between the competent authorities of the Contracting Parties under Article 13.

Article 12

Other international agreements or arrangements

This article may not be required

The possibilities of assistance provided by this Agreement do not limit, nor are they limited by, those contained in existing international agreements or other arrangements between the Contracting Parties which relate to co-operation in tax matters.

Article 13

Mutual Agreement Procedure

1. Where difficulties or doubts arise between two or more Contracting Parties regarding the implementation or interpretation of the Agreement, the competent authorities of those Contracting Parties shall endeavour to resolve the matter by mutual agreement.

2. In addition to the agreements referred to in paragraph 1, the competent authorities of two or more Contracting Parties may mutually agree:
a) on the procedures to be used under Articles 5 and 6;
b) on the language to be used in making and responding to requests in accordance with Article 11.

1. Where difficulties or doubts arise between the Contracting Parties regarding the implementation or interpretation of the Agreement, the competent authorities shall endeavour to resolve the matter by mutual agreement.

2. In addition to the agreements referred to in paragraph 1, the competent authorities of the Contracting Parties may mutually agree on the procedures to be used under Articles 5 and 6.

3. The competent authorities of the Contracting Parties may communicate with each other directly for purposes of reaching agreement under this Article.

4. Any agreement between the competent authorities of two or more Contracting Parties shall be effective only between those Contracting Parties.

4. The paragraph would not be necessary.

5. The Contracting Parties may also agree on other forms of dispute resolution.

Article 14

Depositary's functions

The article would be unnecessary

1. The depositary shall notify all Contracting Parties of:

a. the deposit of any instrument of ratification, acceptance or approval of this Agreement;

b. any date of entry into force of this Agreement in accordance with the provisions of Article 15;

c. any notification of termination of this Agreement;

d. any other act or notification relating to this Agreement.

2. At the request of one or more of the competent authorities of the Contracting Parties, the depositary may convene a meeting of the competent authorities or their representatives, to discuss significant matters related to interpretation or implementation of the Agreement.

Article 15

Entry into Force

1. This Agreement is subject to ratification, acceptance or approval. Instruments of ratification, acceptance or approval shall be submitted to the depositary of this Agreement.	1. This Agreement is subject to ratification, acceptance or approval by the Contracting Parties, in accordance with their respective laws. Instruments of ratification, acceptance or approval shall be exchanged as soon as possible.
2. Each Contracting Party shall specify in its instrument of ratification, acceptance or approval vis-à-vis which other party it wishes to be bound by this Agreement. The Agreement shall enter into force only between Contracting Parties that specify each other in their respective instruments of ratification, acceptance or approval.	2. This Agreement shall enter into force on 1 January 2004 with respect to exchange of information for criminal tax matters. The Agreement shall enter into force on 1 January 2006 with respect to all other matters covered in Article 1.
3. This Agreement shall enter into force on 1 January 2004 with respect to exchange of information for criminal tax matters. The Agreement shall enter into force on 1 January 2006 with respect to all other matters covered in Article 1. For each party depositing an instrument after such entry into force, the Agreement shall enter into force on the 30th day following the deposit of both instruments.	
4. Unless an earlier date is agreed by the Contracting Parties, the provisions of this Agreement shall have effect	3. The provisions of this Agreement shall have effect: - with respect to criminal tax

- with respect to criminal tax matters for tax able periods beginning on or after 1 January 2004 or, where there is no taxable period, for all charges to tax arising on or after 1 January 2004;
- with respect to all other matters described in Article 1 for all taxable periods beginning on or after January 1 2006 or, where there is no taxable period, for all charges to tax arising on or after 1 January 2006.

In cases addressed in the third sentence of paragraph 3, the Agreement shall take effect for all taxable periods beginning on or after the sixtieth day following entry into force, or where there is no taxable period for all charges to tax arising on or after the sixtieth day following entry into force.

matters for taxable periods beginning on or after 1 January 2004 or, where there is no taxable period, for all charges to tax arising on or after 1 January 2004;
-with respect to all other matters described in Article 1 for all taxable periods beginning on or after January 1 2006 or, where there is no taxable period, for all charges to tax arising on or after 1 January 2006.

Article 16

Termination

1. Any Contracting Party may terminate this Agreement vis-à-vis any other Contracting Party by serving a notice of termination either through diplomatic channels or by letter to the competent authority of the other Contracting Party. A copy shall be provided to the depositary of the Agreement.

2. Such termination shall become effective on the first day of the month following the expiration of a period of six months after the date of receipt of the notification by

Termination

1. Either Contracting Party may terminate the Agreement by serving a notice of termination either through diplomatic channels or by letter to the competent authority of the other Contracting Party.

2. Such termination shall become effective on the first day of the month following the expiration of a period of six months after the date of receipt of notice of

the depositary.

3. Any Contracting Party that terminates the Agreement shall remain bound by the provisions of Article 8 with respect to any information obtained under the Agreement.

termination by the other Contracting Party.

3. A Contracting Party that terminates the Agreement shall remain bound by the provisions of Article 8 with respect to any information obtained under the Agreement.

In witness whereof, the undersigned, being duly authorised thereto, have signed the Agreement.

III. COMMENTARY

Title and Preamble

1. The preamble sets out the general objective of the Agreement. The objective of the Agreement is to facilitate exchange of information between the parties to the Agreement. The multilateral and the bilateral versions of the preamble are identical except that the multilateral version refers to the signatories of the Agreement as "Parties" and the bilateral version refers to the signatories as the "Government of ______." The formulation "Government of _____" in the bilateral context is used for illustrative purposes only and countries are free to use other wording in accordance with their domestic requirements or practice.

Article 1 (Object and Scope of Agreement)

2. Article 1 defines the scope of the Agreement, which is the provision of assistance in tax matters through exchange of information that will assist the Contracting Parties to administer and enforce their tax laws.

3. The Agreement is limited to exchange of information that is foreseeably relevant to the administration and enforcement of the laws of the applicant Party concerning the taxes covered by the Agreement. The standard of foreseeable relevance is intended

to provide for exchange of information in tax matters to the widest possible extent and, at the same time, to clarify that Contracting Parties are not at liberty to engage in fishing expeditions or to request information that is unlikely to be relevant to the tax affairs of a given taxpayer. Parties that choose to enter into bilateral agreements based on the Agreement may agree to an alternative formulation of this standard, provided that such alternative formulation is consistent with the scope of the Agreement.

4. The Agreement uses the standard of foreseeable relevance in order to ensure that information requests may not be declined in cases where a definite assessment of the pertinence of the information to an on-going investigation can only be made following the receipt of the information. The standard of foreseeable relevance is also used in the Joint Council of Europe/OECD Convention on Mutual Administrative Assistance in Tax Matters.

5. The last sentence of Article 1 ensures that procedural rights existing in the requested Party will continue to apply to the extent they do not unduly prevent or delay effective exchange of information. Such rights may include, depending on the circumstances, a right of notification, a right to challenge the exchange of information following notification or rights to challenge information gathering measures taken by the requested Party. Such procedural rights and safeguards also include any rights secured to persons that may flow from relevant international agreements on human rights and the expression "unduly prevent or delay" indicates that such rights may take precedence over the Agreement.

6. Article 1 strikes a balance between rights granted to persons in the requested Party and the need for effective exchange of information. Article 1 provides that rights and safeguards are not overridden simply because they could, in certain circumstances, operate to prevent or delay effective exchange of information. However, Article 1 obliges the requested Party to ensure that any such rights and safeguards are not applied in a manner that unduly prevents or delays effective exchange of information. For instance, a bona fide procedural safeguard in the requested Party may delay a response to an information request. However, such a delay should not be considered as "unduly preventing or delaying " effective exchange of information unless the delay is such that it calls into

question the usefulness of the information exchange agreement for the applicant Party. Another example may concern notification requirements. A requested Party whose laws require prior notification is obliged to ensure that its notification requirements are not applied in a manner that, in the particular circumstances of the request, would frustrate the efforts of the party seeking the information. For instance, notification rules should permit exceptions from prior notification (*e.g.*, in cases in which the information request is of a very urgent nature or the notification is likely to undermine the chance of success of the investigation conducted by the applicant Party). To avoid future difficulties or misunderstandings in the implementation of an agreement, the Contracting Parties should consider discussing these issues in detail during negotiations and in the course of implementing the agreement in order to ensure that information requested under the agreement can be obtained as expeditiously as possible while ensuring adequate protection of taxpayers' rights.

Article 2 (Jurisdiction)

7. Article 2 addresses the jurisdictional scope of the Agreement. It clarifies that a requested Party is not obligated to provide information which is neither held by its authorities nor is in the possession or control of persons within its territorial jurisdiction. The requested Party's obligation to provide information is not, however, restricted by the residence or the nationality of the person to whom the information relates or by the residence or the nationality of the person in control or possession of the information requested. The term "possession or control" should be construed broadly and the term "authorities" should be interpreted to include all government agencies. Of course, a requested Party would nevertheless be under no obligation to provide information held by an "authority" if the circumstances described in Article 7 (Possibility of Declining a Request) were met.

Article 3 (Taxes Covered)

Paragraph 1

8. Article 3 is intended to identify the taxes with respect to which the Contracting Parties agree to exchange information in accordance with the provisions of the Agreement. Article 3

appears in two versions: a multilateral version and a bilateral version. The multilateral Agreement applies to taxes on income or profits, taxes on capital, taxes on net wealth, and estate, inheritance or gift taxes. "Taxes on income or profits" includes taxes on gains from the alienation of movable or immovable property. The multilateral Agreement, in sub-paragraph b), further permits the inclusion of taxes imposed by or on behalf of political sub-divisions or local authorities. Such taxes are covered by the Agreement only if they are listed in the instrument of ratification, approval or acceptance.

9. Bilateral agreements will cover, at a minimum, the same four categories of direct taxes (*i.e.*, taxes on income or profits, taxes on capital, taxes on net wealth, and estate, inheritance or gift taxes) unless both parties agree to waive one or more of them. A Contracting Party may decide to omit any or all of the four categories of direct taxes from its list of taxes to be covered but it would nevertheless be obligated to respond to requests for information with respect to the taxes listed by the other Contracting Party (assuming the request otherwise satisfies the terms of the Agreement). The Contracting Parties may also agree to cover taxes other than the four categories of direct taxes. For example, Contracting Party A may list all four direct taxes and Contracting Party B may list only indirect taxes. Such an outcome is likely where the two Contracting Parties have substantially different tax regimes.

Paragraph 2

10. Paragraph 2 of the multilateral version provides that the Contracting Parties may agree to extend the Agreement to cover indirect taxes. This possible extension is consistent with Article 26 of the OECD Model Convention on Income and on Capital, which now covers "taxes of every kind and description." There is no equivalent to paragraph 2 in the bilateral version because the issue can be addressed under paragraph 1. Any agreement to extend the Agreement to cover indirect taxes should be notified to the depositary. Paragraph 2 of the bilateral version is discussed below together with paragraph 3 of the multilateral version.

Paragraph 3

11. Paragraph 3 of the multilateral version and paragraph 2 of the bilateral version address "identical taxes", "substantially similar taxes" and further contain a rule on the expansion or modification of the taxes covered by the Agreement. The Agreement applies automatically to all "identical taxes". The Agreement applies to "substantially similar taxes" if the competent authorities so agree. Finally, the taxes covered by the Agreement can be expanded or modified if the Contracting Parties so agree.

12. The only difference between paragraph 3 of the multilateral version and paragraph 2 of the bilateral version is that the former refers to the date of entry into force whereas the later refers to the date of signature. The multilateral version refers to entry into force because in the multilateral context there might be no official signing of the Agreement between the Contracting Parties.

13. In the multilateral context the first sentence of paragraph 3 is of a declaratory nature only. The multilateral version lists the taxes by general type. Any tax imposed after the date of signature or entry into force of the Agreement that is of such a type is already covered by operation of paragraph 1. The same holds true in the bilateral context, if the Contracting Parties choose to identify the taxes by general type. Certain Contracting Parties, however, may wish to identify the taxes to which the Agreement applies by specific name (*e.g.*, the Income Tax Act of 1999). In these cases, the first sentence makes sure that the Agreement also applies to taxes that are identical to the taxes specifically identified.

14. The meaning of "identical" should be construed very broadly. For instance, any replacement tax of an existing tax that does not change the nature of the tax should be considered an "identical" tax. Contracting Parties seeking to avoid any uncertainty regarding the interpretation of "identical" versus "substantially similar" may wish to delete the second sentence and to include substantially similar taxes within the first sentence.

Article 4 (Definitions)

Paragraph 1

15. Article 4 contains the definitions of terms for purposes of the Agreement. Article 4, paragraph 1, sub-paragraph a) defines the term "Contracting Party". Sub-paragraph b) defines the term "competent authority." The definition recognises that in some Contracting Parties the execution of the Agreement may not fall exclusively within the competence of the highest tax authorities and that some matters may be reserved or may be delegated to other authorities. The definition enables each Contracting Party to designate one or more authorities as being competent to execute the Agreement. While the definition provides the Contracting Parties with the possibility of designating more than one competent authority (for instance, where Contracting Parties agree to cover both direct and indirect taxes), it is customary practice to have only one competent authority per Contracting Party.

16. Sub-paragraph c) defines the meaning of "person" for purposes of the Agreement. The definition of the term "person" given in sub-paragraph c) is intended to be very broad. The definition explicitly mentions an individual, a company and any other body of persons. However, the use of the word "includes" makes clear that the Agreement also covers any other organisational structures such as trusts, foundations, "Anstalten", partnerships as well as collective investment funds or schemes.

17. Foundations, "Anstalten" and similar arrangements are covered by this Agreement irrespective of whether or not they are treated as an "entity that is treated as a body corporate for tax purposes" under sub-paragraph d).

18. Trusts are also covered by this Agreement. Thus, competent authorities of the Contracting Parties must have the authority to obtain and provide information on trusts (such as the identity of settlors, beneficiaries or trustees) irrespective of the classification of trusts under their domestic laws.

19. The main example of a "body of persons" is the partnership. In addition to partnerships, the term "body of persons" also covers less commonly used organisational structures such as unincorporated associations.

20. In most cases, applying the definition should not raise significant issues of interpretation. However, when applying the definition to less commonly used organisational structures,

interpretation may prove more difficult. In these cases, particular attention must be given to the context of the Agreement. *Cf. Article 4, paragraph 2*. The key operational article that uses the term "person" is Article 5, paragraph 4, sub-paragraph b), which provides that a Contracting Party must have the authority to obtain and provide ownership information for all "persons" within the constraints of Article 2. Too narrow an interpretation may jeopardise the object and purposes of the Agreement by potentially excluding certain entities or other organisational structures from this obligation simply as a result of certain corporate or other legal features. Therefore, the aim is to cover all possible organisational structures.

21. For instance an "estate" is recognised as a distinct entity under the laws of certain countries. An "estate" typically denotes property held under the provisions of a will by a fiduciary (and under the direction of a court) whose duty it is to preserve and protect such property for distribution to the beneficiaries. Similarly a legal system might recognise an organisational structure that is substantially similar to a trust or foundation but may refer to it by a different name. The standard of Article 4, paragraph 2 makes clear that where these arrangements exist under the applicable law they constitute "persons" under the definition of sub-paragraph c).

22. Sub-paragraph d) provides the definition of company and is identical to Article 3, paragraph 1 sub-paragraph b) of the OECD Model Convention on Income and on Capital.

23. Sub-paragraphs e) through h) define "publicly traded company" and " collective investment fund or scheme". Both terms are used in Article 5 paragraph 4, sub-paragraph b). Sub-paragraphs e) through g) contain the definition of publicly traded company and sub-paragraph h) addresses collective investment funds or schemes.

24. For reasons of simplicity the definitions do not require a minimum percentage of interests traded (*e.g.* 5 percent of all outstanding shares of a publicly listed company) but somewhat more broadly require that equity interests must be "readily" available for sale, purchase or redemption. The fact that a collective investment fund or scheme may operate in the form of a publicly traded company should not raise any issues because the definitions for both publicly traded company and collective investment fund or scheme are essentially identical.

25. Sub-paragraph e) provides that a "publicly traded company" is any company whose principal class of shares is listed on a recognised stock exchange and whose listed shares can be readily sold or purchased by the public. The term "principal class of shares" is defined in sub-paragraph f). The definition ensures that companies that only list a minority interest do not qualify as publicly traded companies. A publicly traded company can only be a company that lists shares representing both a majority of the voting rights and a majority of the value of the company.

26. The term "recognised stock exchange" is defined in sub-paragraph g) as any stock exchange agreed upon by the competent authorities. One criterion competent authorities might consider in this context is whether the listing rules, including the wider regulatory environment, of any given stock exchange contain sufficient safeguards against private limited companies posing as publicly listed companies. Competent authorities might further explore whether there are any regulatory or other requirements for the disclosure of substantial interests in any publicly listed company.

27. The term "by the public" is defined in the second sentence of sub-paragraph e). The definition seeks to ensure that share ownership is not restricted to a limited group of investors. Examples of cases in which the purchase or sale of shares is restricted to a limited group of investors would include the following situations: shares can only be sold to existing shareholders, shares are only offered to members of a family or to related group companies, shares can only be bought by members of an investment club, a partnership or other association.

28. Restrictions on the free transferability of shares that are imposed by operation of law or by a regulatory authority or are conditional or contingent upon market related events are not restrictions that limit the purchase or sale of shares to a "limited group of investors". By way of example, a restriction on the free transferability of shares of a corporate entity that is triggered by attempts by a group of investors or non-investors to obtain control of a company is not a restriction that limits the purchase or sale of shares to a "limited group of investors".

29. The insertion of "readily" reflects the fact that where shares do not change hands to any relevant degree the rationale for the special mention of publicly traded companies in Article 5,

paragraph 4, sub-paragraph b) does not apply. Thus, for a publicly traded company to meet this standard, more than a negligible portion of its listed shares must actually be traded.

30. Sub-paragraph h) defines a collective investment fund or scheme as any pooled investment vehicle irrespective of legal form. The definition includes collective investment funds or schemes structured as companies, partnerships, trusts as well as purely contractual arrangements. Sub-paragraph h) then defines "public collective investment funds or schemes" as any collective investment fund or scheme where the interests in the vehicle can be readily purchased, sold, or redeemed by the public. The terms "readily" and "by the public" have the same meaning that they have in connection with the definition of publicly traded companies.

31. Sub-paragraphs i, j) and k) are self-explanatory.

32. Sub-paragraph l) defines "information gathering measures." Each Contracting Party determines the form of such powers and the manner in which they are implemented under its internal law. Information gathering measures typically include requiring the presentation of records for examination, gaining direct access to records, making copies of such records and interviewing persons having knowledge, possession, control or custody of pertinent information. Information gathering measures will typically focus on obtaining the requested information and will in most cases not themselves address the provision of the information to the applicant Party.

33. Sub-paragraph m) defines "information". The definition is very broad and includes any fact, statement or record in any form whatever. "Record" includes (but is not limited to): an account, an agreement, a book, a chart, a table, a diagram, a form, an image, an invoice, a letter, a map, a memorandum, a plan, a return, a telegram and a voucher. The term "record' is not limited to information maintained in paper form but includes information maintained in electronic form.

34. Sub-paragraph n) of the multilateral version provides that the depositary of the Agreement is the Secretary General of the OECD.

35. Sub-paragraph o) defines criminal tax matters. Criminal tax matters are defined as all tax matters involving intentional conduct, which is liable to prosecution under the criminal laws of

the applicant Party. Criminal law provisions based on non-intentional conduct (*e.g.* provisions that involve strict or absolute liability) do not constitute criminal tax matters for purposes of the Agreement. A tax matter involves "intentional conduct" if the pertinent criminal law provision requires an element of intent. Sub-paragraph o) does not create an obligation on the part of the applicant Party to prove to the requested Party an element of intent in connection with the actual conduct under investigation.

36. Typical categories of conduct that constitute tax crimes include the wilful failure to file a tax return within the prescribed time period; wilful omission or concealment of sums subject to tax; making false or incomplete statements to the tax or other authorities of facts which obstruct the collection of tax; deliberate omissions of entries in books and records; deliberate inclusion of false or incorrect entries in books and records; interposition for the purposes of causing all or part of the wealth of another person to escape tax; or consenting or acquiescing to an offence. Tax crimes, like other crimes, are punished through fines, incarceration or both.

37. Sub-paragraph p) defines the term "criminal laws" used in sub-paragraph o). It makes clear that criminal laws include criminal law provisions contained in a tax code or any other statute enacted by the applicant Party. It further clarifies that criminal laws are only such laws that are designated as such under domestic law and do not include provisions that might be deemed of a criminal nature for other purposes such as for purposes of applying relevant human rights or other international conventions.

Paragraph 2

38. This paragraph establishes a general rule of interpretation for terms used in the Agreement but not defined therein. The paragraph is similar to that contained in the OECD Model Convention on Income and on Capital. It provides that any term used, but not defined, in the Agreement will be given the meaning it has under the law of the Contracting Party applying the Agreement unless the context requires otherwise. Contracting Parties may agree to allow the competent authorities to use the Mutual Agreement Procedure provided for in Article 13 to agree the meaning of such an undefined term. However, the ability to do so may depend on constitutional or other limitations. In cases

in which the laws of the Contracting Party applying the Agreement provide several meanings, any meaning given to the term under the applicable tax laws will prevail over any meaning that is given to the term under any other laws. The last part of the sentence is, of course, operational only where the Contracting Party applying the Agreement imposes taxes and therefore has "applicable tax laws."

Article 5 (Exchange of Information Upon Request)

Paragraph 1

39. Paragraph 1 provides the general rule that the competent authority of the requested Party must provide information upon request for the purposes referred to in Article 1. The paragraph makes clear that the Agreement only covers exchange of information upon request (*i.e.,* when the information requested relates to a particular examination, inquiry or investigation) and does not cover automatic or spontaneous exchange of information. However, Contracting Parties may wish to consider expanding their co-operation in matters of information exchange for tax purposes by covering automatic and spontaneous exchanges and simultaneous tax examinations.

40. The reference in the first sentence to Article 1 of the Agreement confirms that information must be exchanged for both civil and criminal tax matters. The second sentence of paragraph 1 makes clear that information in connection with criminal tax matters must be exchanged irrespective of whether or not the conduct being investigated would also constitute a crime under the laws of the requested Party.

Paragraph 2

41. Paragraph 2 is intended to clarify that, in responding to a request, a Contracting Party will have to take action to obtain the information requested and cannot rely solely on the information in the possession of its competent authority. Reference is made to information "in its possession" rather than "available in the tax files" because some Contracting Parties do not have tax files because they do not impose direct taxes.

42. Upon receipt of an information request the competent authority of the requested Party must first review whether it has

all the information necessary to respond to a request. If the information in its own possession proves inadequate, it must take "all relevant information gathering measures" to provide the applicant Party with the information requested. The term "information gathering measures" is defined in Article 4, paragraph 1, sub-paragraph l). An information gathering measure is "relevant" if it is capable of obtaining the information requested by the applicant Party. The requested Party determines which information gathering measures are relevant in a particular case.

43. Paragraph 2 further provides that information must be exchanged without regard to whether the requested Party needs the information for its own tax purposes. This rule is needed because a tax interest requirement might defeat effective exchange of information, for instance, in cases where the requested Party does not impose an income tax or the request relates to an entity not subject to taxation within the requested Party.

Paragraph 3

44. Paragraph 3 includes a provision intended to require the provision of information in a format specifically requested by a Contracting Party to satisfy its evidentiary or other legal requirements to the extent allowable under the laws of the requested Party. Such forms may include depositions of witnesses and authenticated copies of original records. Under paragraph 3, the requested Party may decline to provide the information in the specific form requested if such form is not allowable under its laws. A refusal to provide the information in the format requested does not affect the obligation to provide the information.

45. If requested by the applicant Party, authenticated copies of unedited original records should be provided to the applicant Party. However, a requested Party may need to edit information unrelated to the request if the provision of such information would be contrary to its laws. Furthermore, in some countries authentication of documents might require translation in a language other than the language of the original record. Where such issues may arise, Contracting Parties should consider discussing these issues in detail during discussions prior to the conclusion of this Agreement.

Paragraph 4

46. Paragraph 4, sub-paragraph a), by referring explicitly to persons that may enjoy certain privilege rights under domestic law, makes clear that such rights can not form the basis for declining a request unless otherwise provided in Article 7. For instance, the inclusion of a reference to bank information in paragraph 4, sub-paragraph a) rules out that bank secrecy could be considered a part of public policy (ordre public). Similarly, paragraph 4, sub-paragraph a) together with Article 7, paragraph 2 makes clear that information that does not otherwise constitute a trade, business, industrial, commercial or professional secret or trade process does not become such a secret simply because it is held by one of the persons mentioned.

47. Sub-paragraph a) should not be taken to suggest that a competent authority is obliged only to have the authority to obtain and provide information from the persons mentioned. Sub-paragraph a) does not limit the obligation imposed by Article 5, paragraph 1.

48. Sub-paragraph a) mentions information held by banks and other financial institutions. In accordance with the Report "*Improving Access to Bank Information for Tax Purposes*"(OECD 2000), access to information held by banks or other financial institutions may be by direct means or indirectly through a judicial or administrative process. As stated in the report, the procedure for indirect access should not be so burdensome and time-consuming as to act as an impediment to access to bank information. Typically, requested bank information includes account, financial, and transactional information as well as information on the identity or legal structure of account holders and parties to financial transactions.

49. Paragraph 4, sub-paragraph a) further mentions information held by persons acting in an agency or fiduciary capacity, including nominees and trustees. A person is generally said to act in a "fiduciary capacity" when the business which he transacts, or the money or property, which he handles, is not his own or for his own benefit, but for the benefit of another person, as to whom he stands in a relation implying and necessitating confidence and trust on the one part and good faith on the other part. The term "agency" is very broad and includes all forms of corporate service providers (*e.g.,* company formation agents, trust companies, registered agents, lawyers).

50. Sub-paragraph b) requires that the competent authorities of the Contracting Parties must have the authority to obtain and provide ownership information. The purpose of the sub-paragraph is not to develop a common "all purpose" definition of ownership among Contracting Parties, but to specify the types of information that a Contracting Party may legitimately expect to receive in response to a request for ownership information so that it may apply its own tax laws, including its domestic definition of beneficial ownership.

51. In connection with companies and partnerships, the legal and beneficial owner of the shares or partnership assets will usually be the same person. However, in some cases the legal ownership position may be subject to a nominee or similar arrangement. Where the legal owner acts on behalf of another person as a nominee or under a similar arrangement, such other person, rather than the legal owner, may be the beneficial owner. Thus the starting point for the ownership analysis is legal ownership of shares or partnership interests and all Contracting Parties must be able to obtain and provide information on legal ownership. Partnership interests include all forms of partnership interests: general or limited or capital or profits. However, in certain cases, legal ownership may be no more than a starting point. For example, in any case where the legal owner acts on behalf of any other person as a nominee or under a similar arrangement, the Contracting Parties should have the authority to obtain and provide information about that other person who may be the beneficial owner in addition to information about the legal owner. An example of a nominee is a nominee shareholding arrangement where the legal title-holder that also appears as the shareholder of record acts as an agent for another person. Within the constraints of Article 2 of the Agreement, the requested Party must have the authority to provide information about the persons in an ownership chain.

52. In connection with trusts and foundations, sub-paragraph b) provides specifically the type of identity information the Contracting Parties should have the authority to obtain and provide. This is not limited to ownership information. The same rules should also be applied to persons that are substantially similar to trusts or foundations such as the "Anstalt." Therefore, a Contracting Party should have, for example, the authority to obtain and provide information on the identity of the settlor and

the beneficiaries and persons who are in a position to direct how assets of the trust or foundation are to be dealt with.

53. Certain trusts, foundations, "Anstalten" or similar arrangements, may not have any identified group of persons as beneficiaries but rather may support a general cause. Therefore, ownership information should be read to include only identifiable persons. The term "foundation council" should be interpreted very broadly to include any person or body of persons managing the foundation as well as persons who are in a position to direct how assets of the trust or foundation are to be dealt with.

54. Most organisational structures will be classified as a company, a partnership, a trust, a foundation or a person similar to a trust or foundation. However, there might be entities or structures for which ownership information might be legitimately requested but that do not fall into any of these categories. For instance, a structure might, as a matter of law, be of a purely contractual nature. In these cases, the Contracting Parties should have the authority to obtain and provide information about any person with a right to share in the income or gain of the structure or in the proceeds from any sale or liquidation.

55. Sub-paragraph b) also provides that a requested Party must have the authority to obtain and provide ownership information for all persons in an ownership chain provided, as is set out in Article 2, the information is held by the authorities of the requested State or is in the possession or control of persons who are within the territorial jurisdiction of the requested Party. This language ensures that the applicant Party need not submit separate information requests for each level of a chain of companies or other persons. For instance, assume company A is a wholly-owned subsidiary of company B and both companies are incorporated under the laws of Party C, a Contracting Party of the Agreement. If Party D, also a Contracting Party, requests ownership information on company A and specifies in the request that it also seeks ownership information on any person in A's chain of ownership, Party C in its response to the request must provide ownership information for both company A and B.

56. The second sentence of sub-paragraph b) provides that in the case of publicly traded companies and public collective investment funds or schemes, the competent authorities need only provide ownership information that the requested Party can obtain without disproportionate difficulties. Information can be

obtained only with "disproportionate difficulties" if the identification of owners, while theoretically possible, would involve excessive costs or resources. Because such difficulties might easily arise in connection with publicly traded companies and public collective investment funds or schemes where a true public market for ownership interests exists, it was felt that such a clarification was particularly warranted. At the same time it is recognised that where a true public market for ownership interests exists there is less of a risk that such vehicles will be used for tax evasion or other non-compliance with the tax law. The definitions of publicly traded companies and public collective investment funds or schemes are contained in Article 4, paragraph 1, sub-paragraphs e) through h).

Paragraph 5

57. Paragraph 5 lists the information that the applicant Party must provide to the requested Party in order to demonstrate the foreseeable relevance of the information requested to the administration or enforcement of the applicant Party's tax laws. While paragraph 5 contains important procedural requirements that are intended to ensure that fishing expeditions do not occur, subparagraphs a) through g) nevertheless need to be interpreted liberally in order not to frustrate effective exchange of information. The following paragraphs give some examples to illustrate the application of the requirements in certain situations.

58. Example 1 (sub-paragraph (a))

Where a Party is asking for account information but the identity of the accountholder(s) is unknown, sub-paragraph (a) may be satisfied by supplying the account number or similar identifying information.

59. Example 2 (sub-paragraph (d)) ("is held")

A taxpayer of Country A withdraws all funds from his bank account and is handed a large amount of cash. He visits one bank in both country B and C, and then returns to Country A without the cash. In connection with a subsequent investigation of the taxpayer, the competent authority of Country A sends a request to Country B and to Country C for information regarding bank accounts that may have been opened by the taxpayer at one or both of the banks he visited. Under such circumstances, the competent authority of Country A has grounds to believe that the information is held in Country B or is in the possession or control of a person subject to the jurisdiction of Country B. It also has grounds to believe the same with respect to Country C. Country B (or C) can not decline the request on the basis that Country A has failed to establish that the information "is" in Country B (or C), because it is equally likely that the information is in the other country.

60. Example 3 (sub-paragraph (d))

A similar situation may arise where a person under investigation by Country X may or may not have fled Country Y and his bank account there may or may not have been closed. As long as country X is able to connect the person to Country Y, Country Y may not refuse the request on the ground that Country X does not have grounds for believing that the requested information "is" held in Country Y. Country X may legitimately expect Country Y to make an inquiry into the matter, and if a bank account is found, to provide the requested information.

61. Sub-paragraph d) provides that the applicant Party shall inform the requested Party of the grounds for believing that the information is held in the requested Party or is in the possession or control of a person within the jurisdiction of the requested Party. The term "held in the requested Party" includes information held by any government agency or authority of the requested Party.

62. Sub-paragraph f) needs to be read in conjunction with Article 7, paragraph 1. In particular, see paragraph 77 of the Commentary on Article 7. The statement required under sub-paragraph f) covers three elements: first, that the request is in conformity with the law and administrative practices of the applicant Party; second that the information requested would be obtainable under the laws or in the normal course of administration of the applicant Party if the information were within the jurisdiction of the applicant Party; and third that the information request is in conformity with the Agreement. The "normal course of administrative practice" may include special investigations or special examinations of the business accounts kept by the taxpayer or other persons, provided that the tax authorities of the applicant Party would make similar investigations or examinations if the information were within their jurisdiction.

63. Sub-paragraph g) is explained by the fact that, depending on the tax system of the requested Party, a request for

information may place an extra burden on the administrative machinery of the requested Party. Therefore, a request should only be contemplated if an applicant Party has no convenient means to obtain the information available within its own jurisdiction. In as far as other means are still available in the applicant Party, the statement prescribed in sub-paragraph g) should explain that these would give rise to disproportionate difficulties. In this last case an element of proportionality plays a role. It should be easier for the requested Party to obtain the information sought after, than for the applicant Party. For example, obtaining information from one supplier in the requested Party may lead to the same information as seeking information from a large number of buyers in the applicant Party.

64. It is in the applicant Party's own interest to provide as much information as possible in order to facilitate the prompt response by the requested Party. Hence, incomplete information requests should be rare. The requested Party may ask for additional information but a request for additional information should not delay a response to an information request that complies with the rules of paragraph 5. For possibilities of declining a request, see Article 7 and the accompanying Commentary.

Paragraph 6

65. Paragraph 6 sets out procedures for handling requests to ensure prompt responses. The 90 day period set out in subparagraph b) may be extended if required, for instance, by the volume of information requested or the need to authenticate numerous documents. If the competent authority of the requested Party is unable to provide the information within the 90 day period it should immediately notify the competent authority of the applicant Party. The notification should specify the reasons for not having provided the information within the 90 day period (or extended period). Reasons for not having provided the information include, a situation where a judicial or administrative process required to obtain the information has not yet been completed. The notification may usefully contain an estimate of the time still needed to comply with the request. Finally, paragraph 6 encourages the requested Party to react as promptly as possible and, for instance, where appropriate and practical, even before the time limits established under sub-paragraphs a) and b) have expired.

Article 6 (Tax Examinations Abroad)

Paragraph 1

66. Paragraph 1 provides that a Contracting Party may allow representatives of the applicant Party to enter the territory of the requested Party to interview individuals and to examine records with the written consent of the persons concerned. The decision of whether to allow such examinations and if so on what terms, lies exclusively in the hands of the requested Party. For instance, the requested Party may determine that a representative of the requested Party is present at some or all such interviews or examinations. This provision enables officials of the applicant Party to participate directly in gathering information in the requested Party but only with the permission of the requested Party and the consent of the persons concerned. Officials of the applicant Party would have no authority to compel disclosure of any information in those circumstances. Given that many jurisdictions and smaller countries have limited resources with which to respond to requests, this provision can be a useful alternative to the use of their own resources to gather information. While retaining full control of the process, the requested Party is freed from the cost and resource implications that it may otherwise face. Country experience suggests that tax examinations abroad can benefit both the applicant and the requested Party. Taxpayers could be interested in such a procedure because, it might spare them the burden of having to make copies of voluminous records to respond to a request.

Paragraph 2

67. Paragraph 2 authorises, but does not require, the requested Party to permit the presence of foreign tax officials to be present during a tax examination initiated by the requested Party in its jurisdiction, for example, for purposes of obtaining the requested information. The decision of whether to allow the foreign representatives to be present lies exclusively within the hands of the competent authority of the requested Party. It is understood that this type of assistance should not be requested unless the competent authority of the applicant Party is convinced that the presence of its representatives at the examination in the

requested Party will contribute to a considerable extent to the solution of a domestic tax case. Furthermore, requests for such assistance should not be made in minor cases. This does not necessarily imply that large amounts of tax have to be involved in the particular case. Other justifications for such a request may be the fact that the matter is of prime importance for the solution of other domestic tax cases or that the foreign examination is to be regarded as part of an examination on a large scale embracing domestic enterprises and residents.

68. The applicant Party should set out the motive for the request as thoroughly as possible. The request should include a clear description of the domestic tax case to which the request relates. It should also indicate the special reasons why the physical presence of a representative of the competent authority is important. If the competent authority of the applicant Party wishes the examination to be conducted in a specific manner or at a specified time, such wishes should be stated in the request.

69. The representatives of the competent authority of the applicant Party may be present only for the appropriate part of the tax examination. The authorities of the requested Party will ensure that this requirement is fulfilled by virtue of the exclusive authority they exercise in respect of the conduct of the examination.

Paragraph 3

70. Paragraph 3 sets out the procedures to be followed if a request under paragraph 2 has been granted. All decisions on how the examination is to be carried out will be taken by the authority or the official of the requested Party in charge of the examination.

Article 7 (Possibility of Declining a Request)

71. The purpose of this Article is to identify the situations in which a requested Party is not required to supply information in response to a request. If the conditions for any of the grounds for declining a request under Article 7 are met, the requested Party is given discretion to refuse to provide the information but it should carefully weigh the interests of the applicant Party with the pertinent reasons for declining the request. However, if the requested Party does provide the information the person concerned cannot allege an infraction of the rules on secrecy. In the event that the requested Party declines a request for information it shall

inform the applicant Party of the grounds for its decision at the earliest opportunity.

Paragraph 1

72. The first sentence of paragraph 1 makes clear that a requested Party is not required to obtain and provide information that the applicant Party would not be able to obtain under similar circumstances under its own laws for purposes of the administration or enforcement of its own tax laws.

73. This rule is intended to prevent the applicant Party from circumventing its domestic law limitations by requesting information from the other Contracting Party thus making use of greater powers than it possesses under its own laws. For instance, most countries recognise under their domestic laws that information cannot be obtained from a person to the extent such person can claim the privilege against self-incrimination. A requested Party may, therefore, decline a request if the applicant Party would have been precluded by its own self-incrimination rules from obtaining the information under similar circumstances.

74. In practice, however, the privilege against self-incrimination should have little, if any, application in connection with most information requests. The privilege against self-incrimination is personal and cannot be claimed by an individual who himself is not at risk of criminal prosecution. The overwhelming majority of information requests seek to obtain information from third parties such as banks, intermediaries or the other party to a contract and not from the individual under investigation. Furthermore, the privilege against self-incrimination generally does not attach to persons other than natural persons.

75. The second sentence of paragraph 1 provides that a requested Party may decline a request for information in cases where the request is not made in conformity with the Agreement.

76. Both the first and the second sentence of paragraph 1 raise the question of how the statements provided by the applicant Party under Article 5, paragraph 5, sub-paragraph f) relate to the grounds for declining a request under Article 7, paragraph 1. The provision of the respective statements should generally be sufficient to establish that no reasons for declining a request under Article 7, paragraph 1 exist. However, a requested Party that has

received statements to this effect may still decline the request if it has grounds for believing that the statements are clearly inaccurate.

77. Where a requested Party, in reliance on such statements, provides information to the applicant Party it remains within the framework of this Agreement. A requested Party is under no obligation to research or verify the statements provided by the applicant Party. The responsibility for the accuracy of the statement lies with the applicant Party.

Paragraph 2

78. The first sentence of paragraph 2 provides that a Contracting Party is not obliged to provide information which would disclose any trade, business, industrial, commercial or professional secret or trade process.

79. Most information requests will not raise issues of trade, business or other secrets. For instance, information requested in connection with a person engaged only in passive investment activities is unlikely to contain any trade, business, industrial or commercial or professional secret because such person is not conducting any trade, business, industrial or commercial or professional activity.

80. Financial information, including books and records, does not generally constitute a trade, business or other secret. However, in certain limited cases the disclosure of financial information might reveal a trade business or other secret. For instance, a requested Party may decline a request for information on certain purchase records where the disclosure of such information would reveal the proprietary formula of a product.

81. Paragraph 2 has its main application where the provision of information in response to a request would reveal protected intellectual property created by the holder of the information or a third person. For instance, a bank might hold a pending patent application for safe keeping or a trade process might be described in a loan application. In these cases the requested Party may decline any portion of a request for information that would reveal information protected by patent, copyright or other intellectual property laws.

82. The second sentence of paragraph 2 makes clear that the Agreement overrides any domestic laws or practices that may treat information as a trade, business, industrial, commercial or

professional secret or trade process merely because it is held by a person identified in Article 5, paragraph 4, sub-paragraph a) or merely because it is ownership information. Thus, in connection with information held by banks, financial institutions etc., the Agreement overrides domestic laws or practices that treat the information as a trade or other secret when in the hands of such person but would not afford such protection when in the hands of another person, for instance, the taxpayer under investigation. In connection with ownership information, the Agreement makes clear that information requests cannot be declined merely because domestic laws or practices may treat such ownership information as a trade or other secret.

83. Before invoking this provision, a requested Party should carefully weigh the interests of the person protected by its laws with the interests of the applicant Party. In its deliberations the requested Party should also take into account the confidentiality rules of Article 8.

Paragraph 3

84. A Contracting Party may decline a request if the information requested is protected by the attorney-client privilege as defined in paragraph 3. However, where the equivalent privilege under the domestic law of the requested Party is narrower than the definition contained in paragraph 3 (*e.g.*, the law of the requested Party does not recognise a privilege in tax matters, or it does not recognise a privilege in criminal tax matters) a requested Party may not decline a request unless it can base its refusal to provide the information on Article 7, paragraph 1.

85. Under paragraph 3 the attorney-client privilege attaches to any information that constitutes (1) "confidential communication," between (2) "a client and an attorney, solicitor or other admitted legal representative," if such communication (3) "is produced for the purposes of seeking or providing legal advice" or (4) is "produced for the purposes of use in existing or contemplated legal proceedings."

86. Communication is "confidential" if the client can reasonably have expected the communication to be kept secret. For instance, communications made in the presence of third parties that are neither staff nor otherwise agents of the attorney are not confidential communications. Similarly, communications made to

the attorney by the client with the instruction to share them with such third parties are not confidential communications.

87. The communications must be between a client and an attorney, solicitor or other admitted legal representative. Thus, the attorney-client privilege applies only if the attorney, solicitor or other legal representative is admitted to practice law. Communications with persons of legal training but not admitted to practice law are not protected under the attorney-client privilege rules.

88. Communications between a client and an attorney, solicitor or other admitted legal representative are only privileged if, and to the extent that, the attorney, solicitor or other legal representative acts in his or her capacity as an attorney, solicitor or other legal representative. For instance, to the extent that an attorney acts as a nominee shareholder, a trustee, a settlor, a company director or under a power of attorney to represent the company in its business affairs, he can not claim the attorney-client privilege with respect to any information resulting from and relating to any such activity.

89. Sub-paragraph a) requires that the communications be "produced for the purposes of seeking or providing legal advice." The attorney-client privilege covers communications by both client and attorney provided the communications are produced for purposes of either seeking or providing legal advice. Because the communication must be produced for the purposes of seeking or providing legal advice, the privilege does not attach to documents or records delivered to an attorney in an attempt to protect such documents or records from disclosure. Also, information on the identity of a person, such as a director or beneficial owner of a company, is typically not covered by the privilege.

90. Sub-paragraph b) addresses the case where the attorney does not act in an advisory function but has been engaged to act as a representative in legal proceedings, both at the administrative and the judicial level. Sub-paragraph b) requires that the communications must be produced for the purposes of use in existing or contemplated legal proceedings. It covers communications both by the client and the attorney provided the communications have been produced for use in existing or contemplated legal proceedings.

Paragraph 4

91. Paragraph 4 stipulates that Contracting Parties do not have to supply information the disclosure of which would be contrary to public

policy (ordre public). "Public policy" and its French equivalent "ordre public" refer to information which concerns the vital interests of the Party itself. This exception can only be invoked in extreme cases. For instance, a case of public policy would arise if a tax investigation in the applicant Party were motivated by political or racial persecution. Reasons of public policy might also be invoked where the information constitutes a state secret, for instance sensitive information held by secret services the disclosure of which would be contrary to the vital interests of the requested Party. Thus, issues of public policy should rarely arise in the context of requests for information that otherwise fall within the scope of this Agreement.

Paragraph 5

92. Paragraph 5 clarifies that an information request must not be refused on the basis that the tax claim to which it relates is disputed.

Paragraph 6

93. In the exceptional circumstances in which this issue may arise, paragraph 6 allows the requested Party to decline a request where the information requested by the applicant Party would be used to administer or enforce tax laws of the applicant Party, or any requirements connected therewith, which discriminate against nationals of the requested Party. Paragraph 6 is intended to ensure that the Agreement does not result in discrimination between nationals of the requested Party and identically placed nationals of the applicant Party. Nationals are not identically placed where an applicant state national is a resident of that state while a requested state national is not. Thus, paragraph 6 does not apply to cases where tax rules differ only on the basis of residence. The person's nationality as such should not lay the taxpayer open to any inequality of treatment. This applies both to procedural matters (differences between the safeguards or remedies available to the taxpayer, for example) and to substantive matters, such as the rate of tax applicable.

Article 8 (Confidentiality)

94. Ensuring that adequate protection is provided to information received from another Contracting Party is essential to any exchange of information instrument relating to tax matters. Exchange of information for tax matters must always be coupled with stringent safeguards to ensure that the information is used only for the purposes specified in

Article 1 of the Agreement. Respect for the confidentiality of information is necessary to protect the legitimate interests of taxpayers. Mutual assistance between competent authorities is only feasible if each is assured that the other will treat with proper confidence the information, which it obtains in the course of their co-operation. The Contracting Parties must have such safeguards in place. Some Contracting Parties may prefer to use the term "secret", rather than the term "confidential" in this Article. The terms are considered synonymous and interchangeable for purposes of this Article and Contracting Parties are free to use either term.

95. The first sentence provides that any information received pursuant to this Agreement by a Contracting Party must be treated as confidential. Information may be received by both the applicant Party and the requested Party (see Article 5 paragraph 5).

96. The information may be disclosed only to persons and authorities involved in the assessment or collection of, the enforcement or prosecution in respect of, or the determination of appeals in relation to taxes covered by the Agreement. This means that the information may also be communicated to the taxpayer, his proxy or to a witness. The Agreement only permits but does not require disclosure of the information to the taxpayer. In fact, there may be cases in which information is given in confidence to the requested Party and the source of the information may have a legitimate interest in not disclosing it to the taxpayer. The competent authorities concerned should discuss such cases with a view to finding a mutually acceptable mechanism for addressing them. The competent authorities of the applicant Party need no authorisation, consent or other form of approval for the provision of the information received to any of the persons or authorities identified. The references to "public court proceedings" and to "judicial decisions"' in this paragraph extend to include proceedings and decisions which, while not formally being "judicial", are of a similar character. An example would be an administrative tribunal reaching decisions on tax matters that may be binding or may be appealed to a court or a further tribunal.

97. The third sentence precludes disclosure by the applicant Party of the information to a third Party unless express written consent is given by the Contracting Party that supplied the information. The request for consent to pass on the information to a third party is not to be considered as a normal request for information for the purposes of this Agreement.

Article 9 (Costs)

98. Article 9 allows the Contracting Parties to agree upon rules regarding the costs of obtaining and providing information in response to a request. In general, costs that would be incurred in the ordinary course of administering the domestic tax laws of the requested State would normally be expected to be borne by the requested State when such costs are incurred for purposes of responding to a request for information. Such costs would normally cover routine tasks such as obtaining and providing copies of documents.

99. Flexibility is likely to be required in determining the incidence of costs to take into account factors such as the likely flow of information requests between the Contracting Parties, whether both Parties have income tax administrations, the capacity of each Party to obtain and provide information, and the volume of information involved. A variety of methods may be used to allocate costs between the Contracting Parties. For example, a determination of which Party will bear the costs could be agreed to on a case by case base. Alternatively, the competent authorities may wish to establish a scale of fees for the processing of requests that would take into account the amount of work involved in responding to a request. The Agreement allows for the Contracting Parties or the competent authorities, if so delegated, to agree upon the rules, because it is difficult to take into account the particular circumstances of each Party.

Article 10 (Implementing Legislation)

100. Article 10 establishes the requirement for Contracting Parties to enact any legislation necessary to comply with the terms of the Agreement. Article 10 obliges the Contracting Parties to enact any necessary legislation with effect as of the date specified in Article 15. Implicitly, Article 10 also obliges Contracting Parties to refrain from introducing any new legislation contrary to their obligations under this Agreement.

Article 11 (Language)

101 Article 11 provides the competent authorities of the Contracting Parties with the flexibility to agree on the language(s) that will be used in making and responding to requests, with English and French as options where no other language is chosen. This article may not be necessary in the bilateral context.

Article 12 (Other International Agreements or Arrangements)

102. Article 12 is intended to ensure that the applicant Party is able to use the international instrument it deems most appropriate for obtaining the necessary information. This article may not be required in the bilateral context.

Article 13 (Mutual Agreement Procedure)

Paragraph 1

103. This Article institutes a mutual agreement procedure for resolving difficulties arising out of the implementation or interpretation of the Agreement. Under this provision, the competent authorities, within their powers under domestic law, can complete or clarify the meaning of a term in order to obviate any difficulty.

104. Mutual agreements resolving general difficulties of interpretation or application are binding on administrations as long as the competent authorities do not agree to modify or rescind the mutual agreement.

Paragraph 2

105. Paragraph 2 identifies other specific types of agreements that may be reached between competent authorities, in addition to those referred to in paragraph 1.

Paragraph 3

106. Paragraph 3 determines how the competent authorities may consult for the purposes of reaching a mutual agreement. It provides that the competent authorities may communicate with each other directly. Thus, it would not be necessary to go through diplomatic channels. The competent authorities may communicate with each other by letter, facsimile transmission, telephone, direct meetings, or any other convenient means for purposes of reaching a mutual agreement.

Paragraph 4

107. Paragraph 4 of the multilateral version clarifies that agreements reached between the competent authorities of two or more Contracting Parties would not in any way bind the competent authorities of Contracting Parties that were not parties to the particular agreement. The result is self-evident in the bilateral context and no corresponding provision has been included.

Paragraph 5

108. Paragraph 5 provides that the Contracting Parties may agree to other forms of dispute resolution. For instance, Contracting Parties may stipulate that under certain circumstances, e.g., the failure of resolving a matter through a mutual agreement procedure, a matter may be referred to arbitration.

Article 14 (Depositary's Functions)

109. Article 14 of the multilateral version discusses the functions of the depositary. There is no corresponding provision in the bilateral context.

Article 15 (Entry into Force)

Paragraph 1

110. Paragraph 1 of the bilateral version contains standard language used in bilateral treaties. The provision is similar to Article 29, paragraph 1 of the OECD Model Convention on Income and on Capital.

Paragraph 2

111. Paragraph 2 of the multilateral version provides that the Agreement will enter into force only between those Contracting Parties that have mutually stated their intention to be bound vis-à-vis the other Contracting Party. There is no corresponding provision in the bilateral context.

Paragraph 3

112. Paragraph 3 differentiates between exchange of information in criminal tax matters and exchange of information in all other tax matters. With regard to criminal tax matters the Agreement will enter

into force on January 1, 2004. Of course, where Contracting Parties already have in place a mechanism (*e.g.*, a mutual legal assistance treaty) that allows information exchange on criminal tax matters consistent with the standard described in this Agreement, the January 1, 2004 date would not be relevant. See Article 12 of the Agreement and paragraph 5 of the introduction. With regard to all other matters the Agreement will enter into force on January 1, 2006. The multilateral version also provides a special rule for parties that subsequently want to make use of the Agreement. In such a case the Agreement will come into force on the 30th day after deposit of both instruments. Consistent with paragraph 2, the Agreement enters into force only between two Contracting Parties that mutually indicate their desire to be bound vis-à-vis another Contracting Party. Thus, both parties must deposit an instrument unless one of the parties has already indicated its desire to be bound vis-à-vis the other party in an earlier instrument. The 30-day period commences when both instruments have been deposited.

Paragraph 4

113. Paragraph 4 contains the rules on the effective dates of the Agreement. The rules are identical for both the multilateral and the bilateral version. Contracting Parties are free to agree on an earlier effective date.

114. The rules of paragraph 4 do not preclude an applicant Party from requesting information that precedes the effective date of the Agreement provided it relates to a taxable period or chargeable event following the effective date. A requested Party, however, is not in violation of this Agreement if it is unable to obtain information predating the effective date of the Agreement on the grounds that the information was not required to be maintained at the time and is not available at the time of the request.

Article 16 (Termination)

115. Paragraphs 1 and 2 address issues concerning termination. The fact that the multilateral version speaks of "termination" rather than denunciation reflects the nature of the multilateral version as more of a bundle of identical bilateral treaties rather than a "true" multilateral agreement.

116. Paragraph 3 ensures that the obligations created under Article 8 survive the termination of the Agreement.

Enabling Effective Exchange of Information: Availability and Reliability Standard

The Joint Ad Hoc Group on Accounts (JAHGA) Report

A. Introduction

1. Exchange of information for tax purposes is effective when reliable information, foreseeably relevant to the tax requirements of a requesting jurisdiction is available, or can be made available, in a timely manner and there are legal mechanisms that enable the information to be obtained and exchanged. This requires clear rules regarding the maintenance of accounting records and access to such records.

2. There are a number of ways in which the availability of, and access to, accounting records can be ensured. This paper concentrates on the outcome of ensuring access to and the availability of reliable and foreseeably relevant information.

3. The paper has been developed jointly by OECD and non-OECD countries[48] (the "Participating Partners") through their co-operation in the Global Forum Joint Ad Hoc Group on Accounts ("JAHGA"). The JAHGA participants consisted of representatives from: Antigua and Barbuda, Aruba, The Bahamas, Bahrain, Belize, Bermuda, British Virgin Islands, Canada, Cayman Islands, Cook Islands, France, Germany, Gibraltar, Grenada, Guernsey, Ireland, Isle of Man, Italy, Japan, Jersey, Malta, Mauritius, Mexico, Netherlands, Netherlands Antilles, New Zealand, Panama, Saint Kitts and Nevis, Saint Lucia, Saint Vincent and the Grenadines, Samoa, Seychelles, Slovak Republic, Spain, Sweden, United Kingdom and the United States.

48 Reference in this document to "countries" should be taken to apply equally to "territories" or "jurisdictions."

4. The delegates of the Participating Partners developed this paper with the understanding that they were on a common ground and with the common aim of fostering a transparent and well regulated global financial system based on common standards, which seeks the participation of all countries that offer themselves as responsible jurisdictions in a global economy.

5. The paper is built upon the idea that the rules and standards implemented by all Participating Partners must ensure effective exchange of information. The mechanisms must therefore be simple, reliable and equitable.

6. Moreover, no rule or standard should result in creating a competitive advantage for one type of entity or arrangement over another. The paper therefore seeks to apply to all entities and arrangements relevant to this exercise and any reference to the term "Relevant Entities and Arrangements" in this paper is meant to include (i) a company, foundation, Anstalt and any similar structure, (ii) a partnership[49] or other body of persons, (iii) a trust[50] or similar arrangement, (iv) a collective investment fund or scheme,[51] and (v) any person holding assets in a fiduciary capacity (*e.g.* an executor in case of an estate).

B. The Availability and Reliability Standard

I. Maintenance of reliable accounting records

7. Reliable accounting records should be kept for all Relevant Entities and Arrangements. To be reliable, accounting records should:

a. correctly explain the transactions of the Relevant Entity or Arrangement;

b. enable the financial position of the Relevant Entity or Arrangement to be determined with reasonable accuracy at any time; and

---

[49] The Annex provides an explanatory note on partnerships.

[50] The Annex provides an explanatory note on trusts.

[51] The term "collective investment fund or scheme" means any pooled investment vehicle irrespective of legal form. See Article 4, paragraph 1, sub-paragraph h) Model Agreement on Exchange of Information on Tax Matters.

c. allow financial statements[52] to be prepared (whether or not there is an obligation to prepare financial statements).

8. To be reliable, accounting records should include underlying documentation, such as invoices, contracts, *etc.* and should reflect details of

a. all sums of money received and expended and the matters in respect of which the receipt and expenditure takes place;

b. all sales and purchases and other transactions; and

c. the assets and liabilities of the Relevant Entity or Arrangement.

9. The extent of accounting records will depend upon the complexity and scale of the activity of the Relevant Entity or Arrangement but shall in any case be sufficient for the preparation of financial statements.[53]

10. In the case of a company, it is the responsibility of the country or territory of incorporation to oblige the company to keep reliable accounting records. This means in particular that this country or territory must have the necessary powers to require the company to produce its accounting records. Notwithstanding the responsibility of the country of incorporation of a company to be able to obtain accounting records, a requesting partner may, for example, also address a request to the country or territory of effective management or administration. In case it receives such a request, the country of effective management or administration must respond directly to the requesting country.

[52] For purposes of this paper the term "financial statements" comprises:

- a statement recording the assets and liabilities of a Relevant Entity or Arrangement at a point in time,
- a statement or statements recording the receipts, payments and other transactions undertaken by a Relevant Entity or Arrangement,
- such notes as may be necessary to give a reasonable understanding of the statements referred to above.

[53] In many cases, Relevant Entities and Arrangements prepare financial statements and in more complex cases financial statements may be an important element in explaining the transactions of a Relevant Entity or Arrangement. Where financial statements exist and are requested by another country, they should be accessible to the requested country's authorities within a reasonable period of time. See also Section IV, below.

11. In the case of a foundation or Anstalt and any similar structure, it is the responsibility of the country under the laws of which such entity is created to oblige the entity to maintain accounting records. Notwithstanding the responsibility of the country or territory of formation, a requesting partner may, for example, also address a request to the country of effective management.

12. In the case of trusts and partnerships, the governing trust, partnership or other applicable law should result in record keeping requirements and countries should have the power to obtain that information. However, in certain jurisdictions record keeping requirements may not exist in relation to certain types of trusts, such as implied and constructive trusts, which are not used in commercial applications. The principles outlined in this paragraph should also apply to estates and other situations where persons hold assets in a fiduciary capacity.

13. The principles applicable to collective investment funds or schemes generally follow their legal classification. Thus, for instance, the rules on companies apply to any collective investment fund or scheme operated in the legal form of a company. Furthermore, as collective investment funds are typically regulated, the jurisdiction that regulates the fund will generally require that accounting records are kept.

II. Accounting record retention period

14. Accounting records need to be kept for a minimum period that should be equal to the period established in this area by the Financial Action Task Force. This period is currently five years. A five-year period represents a minimum period and longer periods are, of course, also acceptable.

III. Ensuring the maintenance of reliable accounting records

15. Countries should have in place a system or structure that ensures that accounting records, consistent with the standards set out in the first three paragraphs of B.I (Maintenance of reliable accounting records), are kept. There are different ways in which this objective can be achieved. Countries should consider which system is most effective and appropriate in the context of their particular circumstances and the discussion below is intended to give examples of possible approaches without trying to be exhaustive. The design of the system and its composition are for each country to decide. Note that some of the approaches described below may not be sufficient on their own and may need to be combined with others to achieve the intended objective.

16. <u>*Governing Law (including company law, partnership law, trust law) and Commercial Law*</u>. For instance, the governing law may require the maintenance of reliable accounting records and provide for effective sanctions where this requirement is not met. Such sanctions may include effective penalties imposed on the Relevant Entity or Arrangement and persons responsible for its actions (*e.g.* directors, trustees, partners) and may, where possible and appropriate, include striking off an entity from a company or similar registry.

17. The applicable law may further require the preparation of financial statements and may require a person such as a company director to attest that the financial statements provide a full and fair picture of the affairs of the Relevant Entity or Arrangements. The law may further require that the financial statements be audited. Furthermore, financial statements may have to be filed with a governmental authority or the law may require the filing of a statement to the effect that complete and reliable accounting records are being maintained and can be inspected upon request. Filing of incorrect information would typically trigger significant penalties or other sanctions. Such mechanisms either implicitly or explicitly assist in ensuring that reliable accounting records exist and enhance the integrity and credibility of the information.

18. <u>*Financial Regulatory Law, Anti-money Laundering Law or other Regulatory Law*</u>. Financial regulatory law may impose the obligation to keep reliable accounting records on all regulated entities and a failure to comply with such obligation may trigger significant penalties such as monetary fines and a possible withdrawal of the authorisation to conduct the financial business in question. Furthermore, anti-money laundering rules typically require the retention of transactional records by all persons covered by the legislation or implementing regulations and violations of these obligations trigger a range of penalties which may include criminal law consequences.

19. The keeping of reliable accounting records may also result from the regulation of company and trust service providers. For instance, a company and trust service provider acting as a trustee or company director or manager may be required to keep adequate and orderly accounting records for all trust or company transactions. A screening process focused on the integrity and competence of persons wishing to perform company and trust services along with adequate ongoing supervision of their activities, significant monetary fines for rule violations and the possibility that a license may be withdrawn could be effective ways of ensuring that reliable accounting records are kept.

20. *Tax Law*. Tax laws will typically require that taxpayers keep reliable accounting records. Tax laws contain a range of sanctions in cases where reliable accounting records are not kept (*e.g.* interest charges, monetary penalties, assessment on the basis of an estimated tax, possible criminal consequences).

21. *Effective Self-executing Mechanisms*. In certain cases the maintenance of reliable accounting records may also be helped through the respective interests of the parties involved. For example, in the area of collective investment funds, commercial realities may be such that, in practice, a fund would not be able to attract and retain investor funds if it did not have in place a system to ensure the maintenance of reliable accounting records.

IV. Access to accounting records

22. Where accounting records are requested by another party they should be accessible to the requested country's authorities within a reasonable period of time. In particular, the requested country's authorities should have the power to obtain accounting records from any person within their jurisdiction who has possession of, or has control of, or has the ability to obtain, such information. This also means that a requested country should have effective enforcement provisions, including effective sanctions for non-compliance (*e.g.* sanctions for any person who, following notification, refuses to supply information, destroys documents in his possession or transfers them beyond his control). The particular design of enforcement provisions will often be influenced by the approach chosen to ensure that reliable accounting records are kept.[54]

23. This obligation does not necessarily entail a requirement to keep accounting records onshore. However, where accounting records are permitted to be kept offshore, countries should have a system in place that permits their authorities to gain access to such records in a timely fashion.

[54] The principles outlined in this paragraph should also apply to the ability of countries to obtain financial statements, where financial statements exist.

Appendix to the Final JAHGA Paper
Explanatory Note on Trusts

1. Definitions of a trust are to be found in the domestic trust law of those jurisdictions where such laws exist. Alternatively the definition can be taken from the Hague Convention on the Recognition of Trusts.

2. As an example of a definition incorporated in a trust law, the following is taken from the Trusts (Guernsey) Law, 1989, which mirrors the definition in the Jersey (Trusts) Law, 1984:

> "A trust exists if a person (a "trustee") holds or has vested in him, or is deemed to hold or have vested in him, property which does not form, or which has ceased to form, part of his own estate –
>
> a. for the benefit of another person (a "beneficiary"), whether or not yet ascertained or in existence;
>
> b. for any purpose which is not for the benefit only of the trustee."

The Hague Convention on the Law Applicable to Trusts and their Recognition (1985) provides as follows in Article II –

3. "For the purposes of this Convention, the term "trust" refers to legal relationships created .... by a person, the settlor, when assets have been placed under the control of a trustee for the benefit of a beneficiary or for a specified purpose".

4. The definition of a trust whether included in domestic law or in the Hague Convention normally embraces a wide range of types of trust.

5. It is important to remember that a trust is not a legal entity, it is a relationship between juridical persons – settlor, trustee, beneficiary.

Express Trusts

6. These are trusts created voluntarily and intentionally, either orally or in writing –

– inter-vivos by the settlor executing an act or instrument of settlement made between the settlor and the trustees under which the settlor transfers assets to the trustees to hold subject to the terms of the trusts set out therein;

– inter-vivos by the settlor transferring assets to the trustees and the trustees executing a declaration of trust (to which the settlor is not a party) whereby the trustees acknowledge that they hold the assets subject to the terms of the trusts set out in the instrument; or

– on death by the Will of the testator taking effect, whereby the testator's executors are directed to transfer all or part of the testator's estate to trustees (who may be the executors) to hold subject to the trusts set out in the Will.

7. The following are forms of express trusts. Within any trust, different elements of the following may be found.

(a) Bare/Simple Trust

A bare trust is one in which each beneficiary has an immediate and absolute right to both capital and income.

(b) Discretionary Trust

This is a form of trust where the interests of the beneficiaries are not fixed but depend upon the exercise by the trustee of some discretionary powers in their favour. As such it is the most flexible of all trusts.

(c) Interest in Possession Trust

This is a trust where a particular beneficiary (the "life tenant") has a right to receive all the income arising from the trust fund during his life time. The trustee will usually also have a power to apply capital to the life tenant. Often there are successive life interests in favour of an individual and his spouse. On the death of the life tenant the remainder of the trust fund is often held on discretionary trusts for the other beneficiaries.

(d) Fixed Trust

A trust where the interests of beneficiaries are fixed. The trustees will have control over the management of the assets but the interests of the beneficiaries are defined in and by the trust instrument. Typically such a trust may provide an income which is paid, say, to the wife of the settlor and capital to the children on her death.

(e) Accumulation and Maintenance Trust

This form of trust is usually created for the children or grand-children of the settlor, where the trustees have powers during the minority of each beneficiary to pay income in a way beneficial for the upbringing or education of the beneficiary, and to accumulate income not so applied. On attaining a certain age each beneficiary will become entitled to a particular share of the trust fund.

(f) Protective Trust

A trust where the interest of a beneficiary may be reduced or terminated, for example on the happening of events (a common scenario may be if the beneficiary attempts to alienate or dispose of his interest in income or capital).

(g) Employee Share/Options Trusts

Trusts established by institutions in favour of their employees.

(h) Pension Fund Trusts

Trusts established to provide pensions for employees and their dependants.

(i) Charitable Trust

A trust established purely for charitable purposes. In this case there needs to be an enforcer.

(j) Purpose Trust

A trust established for one or more specific purposes. There are no named or ascertainable beneficiaries and there is commonly an enforcer to enforce the terms of the purpose trust.

(k) Commercial Trusts

The major applications include –

- unit trusts;
- debenture trusts for bond holders;
- securitisation trusts for balance sheet reconstructions;
- client account trusts for lawyers and other providers of professional services, separate from the provider's own assets;

– retention fund trusts, pending completion of contracted work.

Implied Trusts

8. A trust can also arise from an oral declaration or by conduct and may be deemed by the Court to have been created in certain circumstances. On account of their very nature there are no formal requirements for those trusts. Usually the existence of such trusts is only recognised as a result of legal action.

Resulting Trusts

9. Both express and implied trusts require an intention for their creation. A resulting trust arises where the intention is absent and yet the legal title to property is transferred from one person to another. By way of example, where X transfers £100 to Y at the same time as executing an Express Trust in respect of £80, only the balance of £20 is held on a Resulting Trust to be retransferred back to X. In this situation, in the absence of intention, the beneficial ownership remains with the Transferor.

Constructive Trusts

10. Constructive Trusts are those Trusts that arise in circumstances in which it would be unconscionable or inequitable for a person holding the property to keep it for his own use and benefit absolutely. A constructive trust can arise in a number of differing scenarios covering a broad spectrum of activity. The proceeds of criminal activity can be traced into the hands of the recipient's bankers who, once alerted, would hold them as constructive trustee on behalf of those to whom they actually belong.

11. Trusts may also be classified according to why they are created and may include –

– private trusts – made for the benefit of specific private individuals, or a class thereof;

– public trusts – made for the benefit of the public at large, or a section of the public – for example a charitable trust established to relieve poverty, to advance education or to promote religion;

– purpose trusts (see above).

12. This brief, and limited, description of trusts shows that the concept encompasses a wide variety of arrangements. Essential to them all is that legal ownership and control is passed from the settlor to the trustee.

Explanatory Note on Partnerships

Partnerships exist under the laws of many jurisdictions. While definitions vary among jurisdictions, a common characteristic is that a partnership is an association of two or more persons, formed by agreement to jointly pursue a common objective.

In many common law jurisdictions an essential element of a partnership is that the "common objective" must consist of the carrying on of a business for profit. For instance, Section 1 of the UK Partnership Act 1890 defines a partnership as "the relation which subsists between persons carrying on a business in common with a view of profit." Identical definitions are found in the laws of Australia, Bermuda, Canada, Ireland and many other jurisdictions that have followed UK legal principles. Very similarly, under the U.S. Uniform Partnership Act[55] a partnership is defined as "an association of two or more persons to carry on as co-owners a business for profit."

In many civil law countries, such as Germany or Spain, partnerships may be formed to pursue a common objective either of a business or a non-business nature and a profit motive is not a necessary prerequisite.

The laws of many jurisdictions distinguish between general partnerships and limited partnerships. The most noteworthy features of a general partnership are that all its partners have unlimited liability for the financial obligations of the partnership and that all partners have the right to participate in the management of the partnership. In contrast, the limited partners of a limited partnership do not have unlimited liability for the financial obligations of the partnership and they do not have a statutory right to manage the affairs of the partnership. The liability of limited partners for the obligations of the partnership is limited to the amount of their capital contribution required under the terms of the partnership agreement and the applicable law. Furthermore, limited partnerships must have at least one general partner with unlimited liability.

---

[55] Uniform Partnership Act, Sec. 6(1); Revised Uniform Partnership Act, Sec. 101(4).

The laws of many jurisdictions also recognise other types of partnerships. One such type is the limited liability partnership. A limited liability partnership is a hybrid of a general and a limited partnership. It typically allows participation in the management of the partnerships by all partners but limits the liability of the partners for financial obligations of the partnership. The limited liability partnership itself is liable for all its debts and obligations and its liability is limited to its own funds. The partners are shielded from all liabilities, other than liabilities arising from their own acts.

The 2006 OECD Manual on Information Exchange – Module on General and Legal Aspects of Exchange of Information

1. The goal of the present manual is to provide officials dealing with exchange of information for tax purposes with an overview of the operation of exchange of information provisions and some technical and practical guidance, in order to improve the efficiency of such exchanges. The Manual may also be helpful in connection with training programs and may provide useful guidance to tax administrations in designing or revising their own manuals.

2. This Manual follows a modular approach. This first module discusses general and legal aspects of exchange of information. The other modules discuss particular aspects of exchange of information. The specific modules deal with the following subjects:

- Exchange of information on request.
- Spontaneous information exchange.
- Automatic (or routine) exchange of information.
- Industry-wide exchange of information.
- Simultaneous tax examinations.
- Tax examinations abroad.
- Country profiles regarding information exchange.
- Information Exchange Instruments and Models.

3. Some of these modules may not be relevant for certain countries. For instance, Article 26 of the OECD Model Convention on Income and Capital ("Model Convention") provides for a framework

within which contracting parties[56] can exchange information on request, as well as on a spontaneous and an automatic basis. The 2002 Model Agreement on Exchange of Information on Tax Matters ("Model Agreement") is focused on information exchange upon request and does not cover spontaneous or automatic exchange of information.[57] Thus, for a country that exchanges information pursuant to instruments based on the Model Agreement, the modules on spontaneous or automatic exchange of information may not be relevant. The modular structure is designed to address such differences by permitting each country to select and use only those modules relevant to its information exchange policies.

4. The modules focus on information exchange pursuant to instruments based on Article 26 of the Model Convention or on the provisions of the Model Agreement. Other exchange of information instruments or models are mentioned where appropriate. References to the relevant sections of the Council of Europe/OECD Convention on Mutual Administrative Assistance in Tax Matters (the "Council of Europe/OECD Convention") have been incorporated in the footnotes.

5. The Manual discusses information exchange on the basis of the revised text of Article 26 that was agreed by the Committee on Fiscal Affairs in June of 2004. Where the new text differs from the previous version of Article 26 or where relevant additional language has been added to either the Article or its commentary, explanations have been included in accompanying footnotes. As a general matter and as expressly stated in the preliminary remarks of the commentary to Article 26, many of the changes are not intended to alter the substance of the provision but instead to remove doubts as to its proper interpretation.

1. The changing environment

6. The past decades have witnessed an unprecedented liberalisation and globalisation of national economies. An increasing number of countries have removed or limited controls on foreign investment and relaxed or eliminated foreign exchange controls. While tax administrations remain confined to their respective jurisdictions taxpayers operate globally. This imbalance and the differences in national tax systems led OECD to address harmful tax practices by

[56] For the sake of convenience, this Manual uses the term "contracting parties" throughout. The term is intended to include the reference to "Contracting States" found in the Model Convention.

[57] Article 5, paragraph 1 Model Agreement.

focusing on improved transparency and co-operation between tax authorities. This approach has also been shared by a growing number of non-member countries. Countries have increasingly resorted to improved and broadened co-operation in tax matters. In a broader context, the efficient functioning of tax co-operation helps to ensure that taxpayers who have access to cross-border transactions do not also have access to greater tax evasion and avoidance possibilities than taxpayers operating only in their domestic market. Co-operation in tax matters also reflects the basic principle that participation in the global economy carries both benefits and responsibilities. The continued viability of an open world economy depends on international co-operation, including co-operation in tax matters.

7. A key element of international co-operation in tax matters is exchange of information. It is an effective way for countries to maintain sovereignty over their own tax bases and to ensure the correct allocation of taxing rights between tax treaty partners. Exchange of information can be based on a number of different exchange mechanisms. In the context of a comprehensive income tax treaty, exchange of information is often based on a provision modelled on Article 26 of the Model Convention. Outside the context of income tax treaties, exchange of information is increasingly achieved through agreements based on the Model Agreement.

2. Purposes of exchange of information

8. Information is typically exchanged for one of two purposes: First, information is exchanged in order to ascertain the facts in relation to which the rules of an income tax convention are to be applied. Second, information is exchanged with a view to assisting one of the contracting parties in administering or enforcing its domestic tax law. The former case only arises in connection with exchange of information on the basis of a bilateral income tax convention whereas the latter may arise in the context of either a bilateral income tax convention or a bilateral or multilateral mutual assistance or exchange of information agreement.

3. Legal bases of exchange of information

9. There are a number of international legal instruments on the basis of which exchanges of information for tax purposes may take place:

- Bilateral tax conventions which are generally based on the OECD Model Convention on Income and on Capital or the United Nations Model Convention on Income and Capital.

- International instruments designed specifically for administrative assistance purposes in tax matters such as tax information exchange agreements generally based on the 2002 Model Agreement on Exchange of Information on Tax Matters, the Council of Europe/OECD Convention, the Nordic Assistance Convention, the Model Agreement on the Exchange of Tax Information developed by the Inter-American Centre of Tax Administrations (CIAT) or the Model Agreement on Co-operation and Mutual Assistance on Issues of Compliance with Tax Legislation developed by the Russian Federation.

- Within the European Community, the EC Directive on Mutual Assistance (Directive 77/799/EEC as updated), for exchange of information for VAT purposes, Regulation No 1798/2003 and for excise duties, Regulation No 2073/2004.

- International judicial assistance agreements, such as the European Convention on Mutual Assistance in Criminal Matters (as extended to tax matters by the Additional Protocol of 17th March 1978) in cases of prosecution for a tax offence, or the Inter-American Convention on Mutual Assistance in Criminal Matters (as extended by the Optional Protocol of May 23, 1992) in cases of tax crimes.

10. Procedures for providing assistance to foreign jurisdictions may also be established in domestic law. For instance, some countries permit the provision of information to another jurisdiction, subject to certain conditions and safeguards (e.g. reciprocity and confidentiality of information), even in the absence of an international agreement and solely based on their domestic law provisions.

11. When more than one legal instrument may serve as the basis for exchange of information, the problem of overlap is generally addressed within the instruments themselves.[58] Where the applicable instruments contemplate the co-existence of more than one information exchange provision and if there are no domestic rules to the contrary, the competent authorities are generally free to choose the most appropriate instrument on a case-by-case basis. In these cases, it may be desirable for the competent authorities to agree on a common approach for determining which mechanism will be used in the specific circumstances.

58 See Article 27 of the Council of Europe/OECD Convention on Mutual Administrative Assistance in Tax Matters, Article 12 of the Model Agreement, and Paragraph 5.2. of the Commentary on Article 26 of the Model Convention, for EU Member States see also Article 11 of the 1977 EC directive "Applicability of wider-ranging provisions of assistance."

4. Assistance in criminal tax cases

12. Article 26 of the Model Convention and Article 1 of the Model Agreement permit exchange of information in cases that involve criminal tax offences. There may also be - depending on the nature of the legal system of the contracting parties as well as the facts and circumstances of any particular case – alternative legal instruments[59] through which an exchange of information is possible when an inquiry or investigation has criminal aspects and in certain situations countries may have a preference for using such instruments.[60] Unlike the Council of Europe/OECD Convention neither Article 26 of the Model Convention nor the Model Agreement[61] contain a rule that would limit its scope of application depending on the stage of a criminal investigation.[62] Competent authorities may, therefore, request information under Article 26 or the Model Agreement even if criminal tax proceedings have been instituted against a taxpayer, provided, of course, that the information is requested for the purposes covered by Article 26 or the Model Agreement (*see*, paragraph 8 above).

13. As the term "competent authority," usually means the Ministry of Finance or its authorised representative, a judicial authority of one country cannot directly transmit requests for information to another country on the basis of Article 26 or the Model Agreement.

14. Field personnel initiating a request for information from another country should inform their competent authority of the presence of any criminal aspects to the investigation in the first instance. The basis under which the information will be sought will then be determined by the competent authority.

15. If the competent authority requests information of a particular type or in a particular form for criminal tax proceedings, the requested competent

[59] For example, mutual legal assistance treaties or domestic law provisions that may permit exchange of information in criminal matters even in the absence of international agreements.

[60] For example, where the seizure of original records for evidentiary purposes is requested and the requested country can only undertake such measures if the request is based on a mutual legal assistance treaty.

[61] Article 26 of the Model Convention and Article 12 of the Model Agreement only recognise that different exchange of information instruments may coexist.

[62] The Council of Europe/OECD Convention covers information exchange in preparation of criminal proceedings but does not apply once criminal proceedings have begun before a judicial body. See Commentary paragraphs 9 and 56.

authority's ability to comply with the request will depend on the national law of the requested Contracting State.[63]

5. Assistance in tax collection

16. Article 26 of the Model Convention and Article 1 of the Model Agreement do not provide for assistance in tax collection in the sense of empowering the competent authorities to use their powers of collection on behalf of the other contracting party. However, the scope of both the Model Convention and the Model Agreement include information exchange for "collection of taxes" and thus information assisting in the collection of domestic taxes can be exchanged between contracting parties.

17. Article 27 of the Model Convention deals with assistance in the collection of taxes. Furthermore, both the Nordic Assistance Convention and the Joint Council of Europe/OECD Convention include provisions on tax collection. Finally, the EU has developed a Directive on Mutual Assistance for the Recovery of Tax Claims (Directive 76/308/EEC as amended by Directive 2001/44/EEC).

6. Forms of exchange of information

18. Article 26 provides for broad information exchange and does not limit the forms or manner in which information exchange can take place. The main forms of information exchange are: on request, automatic and spontaneous. The Model Agreement only applies to the exchange of information on request, although the contracting parties may agree to expand their co-operation by including the possibility of automatic and spontaneous exchange.[64]

- *Exchange of information on request.* Exchange of information on request refers to a situation where the competent authority of one country asks for particular information from the competent authority of another contracting party.

- *Automatic exchange of information.* Information which is exchanged automatically is typically information comprising many individual cases of the same type, usually consisting of details of income arising from sources in the source country, e.g. interest, dividends, royalties, pensions

[63] For instance, domestic law will determine the types and forms (e.g. deposition of witnesses) of the relevant information gathering measures. See also paragraph 33.

[64] The OECD/Council of Europe Convention contains specific articles dealing with information exchange upon request, spontaneous information exchange, automatic information exchange as well as simultaneous tax examinations and tax examinations abroad. See Articles 5 through 9.

etc. This information is obtained on a routine basis (generally through reporting of the payments by the payer) by the sending country and is thus available for transmission to its treaty partners. Normally, competent authorities interested in automatic exchange will agree in advance as to what type of information they wish to exchange on this basis. To improve the efficiency and effectiveness of automatic exchanges of information the OECD has designed both a standard paper format and a standard electronic format (known as the OECD Standard Magnetic Format or "SMF"). The OECD recommends the use of the SMF and has developed a model memorandum of understanding for automatic exchange of information available for use by any country. The OECD also has designed a "new generation" transmission format for automatic exchange (known as the Standard Transmission Format or "STF") to eventually replace the SMF.

– *Spontaneous exchange of information.* Information is exchanged spontaneously when one of the contracting parties, having obtained information in the course of administering its own tax laws which it believes will be of interest to one of its treaty partners for tax purposes passes on this information without the latter having asked for it. The effectiveness of this form of exchange of information largely depends on the ability of tax inspectors to identify, in the course of an investigation, information that may be relevant for a foreign tax administration. The competent authority of the contracting party that provides information spontaneously should request feedback from the recipient tax administration as it may result in a tax adjustment for the sending contracting party. For instance, a foreign tax administration informed on a spontaneous basis that commission fees were reported to have been paid to one of its residents, may find out that no commission fees were actually paid and it may report this fact to its counterpart who supplied the information. As a result the deduction of the commission fees will be denied and the taxable income adjusted accordingly. Positive feedback also provides an incentive for tax inspectors to continue providing information spontaneously.[65]

19. There are also other forms of exchange of information besides the traditional ones described above:

[65] The OECD/Council of Europe Convention specifically sets forth the circumstances in which the contracting parties should provide information spontaneously. See Article 7(a) through (e).

- *Simultaneous tax examinations*. A simultaneous tax examination is an arrangement by two or more countries to examine simultaneously and independently, each on its territory, the tax affairs of (a) taxpayer(s) in which they have a common or related interest with a view to exchanging any relevant information which they so obtain. The existing differences in statutes of limitations of countries are a major practical consideration in the selection of cases. Such examinations are particularly useful in the area of transfer pricing and in identifying tax evasion schemes involving low tax jurisdictions. The OECD has designed a model agreement for the undertaking of simultaneous tax examinations.

- *Visit of authorised representatives of the competent authorities*. Travel to a foreign jurisdiction for purposes of gathering information for a particular case may be useful in certain circumstances. However, this visit has to be authorised by the foreign jurisdiction (and be permitted by the laws of the sending country), otherwise it would represent a breach of sovereignty. Thus, the decisions on whether or not to authorise such visits, and if so, whether the presence of foreign tax officials should require the consent of the taxpayer (as well as any other terms and conditions for such visits) fall within the sole discretion of individual countries. The tax officials must be authorised representatives of the competent authorities. This presence abroad may occur in different instances. It may be at the request of the country seeking information if it is felt it will facilitate the understanding of the request and the gathering of information. It may be at the initiative of the requested competent authority to reduce the cost and burden of gathering information. In a number of countries, authorised representatives of the competent authorities of the other country may participate in a tax examination and this is often of great value to ascertain a clear picture of business and other relations a resident of a country may have with his foreign associates.

- *Industry-wide exchange of information*: An industry-wide exchange of information does not concern a specific taxpayer but an economic sector as a whole, for instance, the pharmaceutical industry or the oil industry. An industry-wide exchange involves representatives of contracting parties meeting to discuss the way in which a particular economic sector operates, the financing schemes, the way prices are determined, the tax evasion trends identified, etc.

7. The authority to exchange information

20. In most countries relations with other countries fall within the competence of the Ministry of Foreign Affairs. In principle, therefore, official contacts with foreign countries have to be made through diplomatic channels. In the case of information exchange in tax matters, this may, however, not be very practical. The Model Convention and the Model Agreement therefore allow the contracting parties to designate one or more "competent authorities" to deal directly with each other.[66] The competent authority is nominated by the contracting parties and is typically a senior official in the Ministry of Finance (either in the treasury or the tax administration part) or an authorised delegate thereof.

21. The function performed by the competent authority is generally centralised within the Ministry of Finance. The existence of this central body ensures co-operation and the necessary consistency with respect to the exchange of information policy. There are, however, situations in which certain responsibilities of the competent authorities may be delegated to a local level, for instance, in cases of hiring out labour across borders, where direct and speedy contacts between local tax authorities on each side of the border may be the only way in which exchange of information may be effective. This does not imply, however, that the competent authority is no longer involved. Thus, in cases of delegation of functions clear arrangements between the competent authorities will be necessary (e.g. the types of information that may be exchanged, the relevant subject matter area to which this exchange may apply, the process for keeping the competent authorities involved).

22. The OECD maintains a comprehensive list of competent authorities in member (and some non-member) countries.

8. Scope of exchange of information

23. Both Article 26 of the Model Convention and Article 1 of the Model Agreement envisage information exchange to "the widest possible extent". Nevertheless they do not allow "fishing expeditions" *i.e.* speculative requests for information that have no apparent nexus to an open inquiry or investigation. The balance between these two competing considerations is captured in the standard of "foreseeable relevance."[67] The Model Agreement

[66] Article 3(1)(f) Model Convention, 4(1)(b) Model Agreement. This approach is also found in the Council of Europe/OECD Convention, see Article 3(1)(d).

[67] The previous version of Article 26 of the Model Convention used the standard of "necessary". The commentary explains that the change from "necessary" to

specifically sets forth the type of information that a requesting party should provide to "demonstrate the foreseeable relevance of the [requested] information to the request." See Article 5 (5). Article 26 of the Model Convention is less formalistic on this point but a requesting country should nevertheless take into account the items of information identified in the checklist discussed in the module on information upon request. Where a country fails to provide important pieces of information identified on this checklist, a requested competent authority may be led to believe that the request is a fishing expedition.

24. Exchange of information covers all information that is foreseeably relevant to the administration or enforcement of the domestic laws of the contracting parties concerning taxes. In addition, the Model Convention also contemplates information exchange for carrying out the provisions of the convention. Some older income tax treaties limit information exchange to the latter category (*i.e.* information exchange for purposes of applying the convention). However, among OECD members only Switzerland still seeks the inclusion of such a "narrow" exchange of information clause in its bilateral income tax conventions and Switzerland is willing to provide information exchange for domestic law purposes "in cases involving acts of fraud subject to imprisonment according to the laws of both Contracting States".[68]

25. Examples of the scope of Article 26 of the Model Convention are shown in paragraphs 7 and 8 of the Commentary. For instance, for the application of Article 12 of the Model Convention (royalty payments), the country of residence may ask the source country the amount of royalties transmitted to one of its residents, the source country may ask the country of the recipient of the royalties whether he is a resident and whether he is the beneficial owner of the royalties in order to exempt them from withholding. Furthermore, for the application of Articles 7, 9, 23 A and 23 B, information may also be needed for the proper allocation of profits between associated enterprises in different states or between a head office in one state and a permanent establishment in another State. Information necessary for the application of Article 9 also includes information on ownership and control in a foreign person for purposes of establishing whether or not enterprises are associated within the meaning of Article 9.

"foreseeably relevant" was not intended to alter the effect of the provision but was made to better express this balance and to achieve consistency with the Model Agreement. See, paragraphs 4.1 and 5 of the commentary on Article 26. The OECD/Council of Europe Convention also uses the standard of "foreseeably relevant". See Article 4(1).

[68] See the Swiss reservation on Article 26 of the Model Convention.

26. A request for information for the administration or enforcement of the domestic laws either under Article 26 of the Model Convention or Article 1 of the Model Agreement could include any or all of the following items:[69]

- the fiscal residence of an individual or a company;
- the tax status of a legal entity;
- the nature of income in the source country;
- the income and expenses shown on a tax return;
- business records (for instance to determine the amount of commissions paid to a company of another State);
- formation documents of an entity and documents about subsequent changes of shareholders/partners;
- name and address of the entity at the time of formation and all subsequent name and address changes;
- number of entities residing at the same address as the requested entity;
- names and addresses of the directors, managers, and other employees of a company for the relevant years, evidence (contracts and bank statements) of their remuneration, social security-payments and information about their occupation with regard to any other entities;
- banking records;
- accounting records and financial statements;
- copies of invoices, commercial contracts, etc.;
- the price paid for goods in a transaction between independent companies in both States;
- information involving a so-called triangular situation where in

[69] This list is intended to serve as an illustration and is not intended to be exhaustive. Moreover, it should be noted that a request for information is subject to the reciprocity requirements discussed in paragraphs 37 through 39 below.

transactions between two companies, each situated in a contracting party, a company of a third country C (with which neither country A nor B have an information exchange instrument), is interposed. Here, countries A and B may exchange information regarding transactions with the company in country C for the correct taxation of their resident companies;

- prices in general, necessary to check the prices charged by their taxpayers even if there are no business contacts between the taxpayers. For instance, country A may wish to check prices charged by its taxpayers by reference to transfer pricing information on similar transactions in country B, even if there are no business contacts between the respective taxpayers in countries A and B. (see paragraph 8, sub-paragraph c of the Commentary on Article 26 of the Model Convention).

27. The scope of information exchange under the Model Convention and the Model Agreement also permits the exchange of confidential non-taxpayer specific information such as statistics, information about a particular industry, tax evasion trends, administrative interpretations and practices.

9. Persons covered

28. Exchange of information is not limited to information relating to the affairs of residents of the contracting parties.[70] Often, the tax administration of one of the contracting parties will have an interest in receiving information on activities carried on in the other contracting party by a particular person resident in a third country because the tax liability of the latter as a non-resident taxpayer is at issue. However, there are situations where it is conceivable that a contracting party could have an interest in receiving information about a third country resident who is not subject to tax in either of the contracting parties, for instance when this information is relevant to the taxation of a third party who is a taxpayer or resident of the requesting party. Of course, contracting parties cannot provide information on third country residents that is neither held by their authorities nor is in the possession or control of persons within their te4rritorial jurisdiction. While this concept of jurisdictional limitation is implicit in Article 26 it is explicitly stated in Article 2 of the Model Agreement.

Example 1: Bank A, resident in country A has branch operations in both country B and country C. Bank A is engaged in the trading of financial assets

70 See Article 26, paragraph 1 Model Convention, Article 2 Model Convention and Article 1, paragraph 3 of the Council of Europe/OECD Convention.

and its operations in countries A, B, and C are carried out on a highly integrated basis. In the process of determining the taxable income of Bank A's branch in country B, the competent authority of country B requests information from country C relating to the branch operations of Bank A in that country.

Example 2: Component manufacturer A, resident in country A, sells components to a related distributor resident in country B and to unrelated distributors resident in country C. Country C's customs authorities record information on prices charged by A to country C distributors. In connection with an income tax audit of the transfer prices used by the distributor resident in country B, the competent authority of country B requests information from country C relating to the import prices charged by A to country C distributors.

Example 3: A trust has three trustees. Trustees A and B live in Country Y. Trustee C lives in Country Z. Trustees A and B were involved in a transaction but declined to provide, to the tax authorities of Country Y, information concerning the transaction, on the basis that the necessary documents are held by Trustee C, who is refusing to provide them with copies. The competent authority of Country Y asked the competent authority of Country Z to obtain copies of the relevant documentation from Trustee C.

10. Taxes covered

29. The exchange of information under the Model Agreement applies to the administration and enforcement of the taxes covered by the Agreement.[71] The Model Convention uses a different approach and Article 26 also applies to taxes not otherwise covered. Article 26 provides that information exchange applies to taxes "of every kind and description" and goes on to state that the exchange is not limited by Article 2 (Taxes Covered).[72] Thus, Article 26 determines the types of tax for which information can be exchanged rather than Article 2 (Taxes Covered).

Example 1: Country A and country B have entered into a tax convention that follows the OECD Model Convention, *i.e.* while the convention generally only

[71] The Council of Europe/OECD Convention lists the taxes to which it applies in Article 2, paragraph 1.

[72] The vast majority of Double Tax Conventions in force in 2005 do not cover taxes of every kind and description but are limited to the taxes covered by the Convention.

covers taxes on income and capital the exchange of information article contains no such restriction. The competent authority of country A requests certain transactional information about a resident person in country B for the purpose of verifying the sales tax liability of a person resident in country A. The competent authority in country B cannot refuse to comply with the request on the grounds that sales taxes are not otherwise covered by the convention.

Example 2: Same as Example 1 except that country A and country B have entered into a tax information exchange agreement, based on the Model Agreement, that only covers taxes on income and capital. The competent authority in country B does not have to comply with the request because sales taxes are not covered by the agreement.

11. Years covered

30. Time periods during which tax situations may be examined vary from country to country and the beginning of the tax year does not always coincide with the calendar year. Where there is a significant time lag between the time the information is supplied and the year to which the information relates, a statute of limitations issue may arise. The question of whether use of the information is time barred has to be determined by reference to the statute of limitations rules of the country where the information is to be used. In certain countries (*e.g.* France) the sending of a request for information concerning a case subject to a tax examination will suspend the statute of limitations. For questions relating to exchange of information and the issue of entry into force and effective dates, see Article 15 of the Model Agreement and paragraph 10.3. of the Commentary on Article 26.

12. Obligation to exchange information

31. It is important to stress that the exchange of information is mandatory. This is due to the use of the word "shall" in the first sentence of both Article 26 of the Model Convention and Article 1 of the Model Agreement.[73] In connection with the Model Convention the obligation to exchange information is provided by the Article insofar as the taxation under the domestic laws concerned is not contrary to the Convention.

32. The obligation to exchange information is not limited to information contained in the tax files held by a tax administration. Where requested information is not available in the tax files, the requested party must use its information gathering measures to seek to obtain the information

[73] The same formulation is also used in the Council of Europe/OECD Convention. See Article 1, paragraph 1 and Article 4, paragraph 1 and Article 7, paragraph 1.

from the taxpayer(s) or third parties.[74] This may include special investigations or special examination of the business accounts kept by the taxpayer or other persons. Whether or not the requested party has an interest in the information for its own tax purposes is irrelevant. Information must be provided even where the requested party does not need the information for the administration or enforcement of its own tax laws.

33. In some cases, contracting parties may need information in a particular form to satisfy their evidentiary or other legal requirements. Where specifically requested and to the extent allowable under its domestic law the competent authority should try to obtain information in the particular form requested. Such forms typically include depositions of witnesses and authenticated copies of original records.[75]

13. Limitations to exchange of information

34. The legal obligation to supply information is lifted in a limited number of situations. These exceptions are contained in paragraphs 3 through 5 of Article 26 of the Model Convention and in Article 7 of the Model Agreement.[76] In the rare cases where the exceptions apply, the contracting parties are not obligated to provide information. The decision to provide or not to provide the information is then left to the discretion of the requested contracting party. It follows that a competent authority may decide to provide the information even where there is no obligation to do so. If a competent authority does provide the information, it still acts within the framework of the agreement. For instance, where a request relates to information that may involve a trade secret, a competent authority may still provide such information if it feels that the laws and practices of the requesting State together with the confidentiality obligations imposed under Article 26, paragraph 2 of the Model Convention (or Article 8 of the Model Agreement) ensure that the information cannot be used for the unauthorised purposes against which the trade or secrecy rules are intended to protect. If the requested party decides to provide the information it should indicate that a trade or other secret is involved in order to allow the requesting party to take

74 See paragraph 16 of the Commentary on Article 26 of the Model Convention, Article 5, paragraph 2 of the Model Agreement and Article 5 paragraph 2 of the Council of Europe/OECD Convention.

75 See paragraph 10.2. Commentary on Article 26 Model Convention; Article 5(3) Model Agreement and accompanying Commentary.

76 In the Council of Europe/OECD Convention the exceptions are contained in Article 19 and Article 21, paragraph 2.

any additional or special measures as may be appropriate to ensure the strictest confidentiality.

35. The remainder of this section discusses the grounds that can be used for declining information. It also discusses some of the grounds that can not be used for that purpose.

13.1 Tax secrecy

36. Tax secrecy refers to the provisions under domestic law that ensure that information relating to a taxpayer and his affairs remains confidential and is protected from unauthorised disclosure. It is therefore fundamental for the co-operation in matters of information exchange that such confidential information continues to enjoy a similar level of protection when it is exchanged with other countries. For this reason any information supplied by a contracting party must be treated as confidential.[77] Because confidentiality is preserved by the exchange of information instrument and the applicable domestic law in the receiving country the supply of information cannot be declined on the basis that it would contravene domestic tax secrecy rules.

13.2 Reciprocity

37. Reciprocity in relation to exchange of information means that a contracting party, when collecting information for the other contracting party, is obliged only to obtain and provide such information that the requesting party could itself obtain under its own laws in similar circumstances. The Model Convention further provides that a requested party is not obliged to supply information that the requesting party itself could not obtain in the normal course of administration.

38. The underlying idea of the concept of reciprocity is that a contracting party should not be able to take advantage of the information system of the other contracting party if it is wider than its own system.[78] The requested party may refuse to provide information where the requesting party is precluded by law from obtaining or providing information or where the requesting party's administrative practices (*e.g.*, failure to provide sufficient administrative resources) result in a lack of reciprocity. However, it is recognised that too rigorous an application of the principle of reciprocity

---

77 Article 26, paragraph 2; Article 8 of the Model Agreement, Article 22 of the Council of Europe/OECD Convention.

78 See Article 26, paragraph 3, sub-paragraphs a) and b) Model Convention and Article 7, paragraph 1 (first sentence) of the Model Agreement, Article 21, paragraph 2, sub-paragraph a) and c) Council of Europe/OECD Convention.

could frustrate effective exchange of information and that reciprocity should be interpreted in a broad and pragmatic manner. The respective commentaries of the Model Convention and the Model Agreement elaborate further on the principle of reciprocity and its intended application. [79]

39. In practice, it may be difficult for the competent authority to determine in each instance whether the requested party would be able to obtain and provide the requested information under similar circumstances. In order to address this issue, the Model Agreement requires the requesting party to provide a statement confirming that the reciprocity condition is met.[80] Where such a statement is furnished the requested party may decline the request only "if it has grounds for believing that the statements are clearly inaccurate".[81] This mechanism was introduced to facilitate the determination of whether reciprocity was satisfied. The Model Convention does not require the provision of such a statement. However, in cases where a country under its domestic law can only lend assistance if the reciprocity condition is fulfilled it may wish to ask its treaty partner to include a similar statement regarding reciprocity in each request for information. The inclusion of such a statement would then avoid the additional administrative burden that would otherwise result from the competent authority of the requested party having to ask additional questions before the request could be processed.

13.3 Public policy/Ordre Public

40. Another reason for declining to provide information relates to the concept of public policy/ordre public.[82] The Commentary on Article 26 Model Convention (paragraph 19.5[83]) and the Commentary on Article 7

[79] See paragraphs 15 through 15.2 of the Commentary on Article 26 of the Model Convention, paragraphs 72 through 74 of the Commentary on the Model Agreement, paragraphs 189, 195 196 of the commentary on the Council of Europe/OECD Convention The previous version of the commentary on Article 26 contained a less detailed discussion of the principle of reciprocity. However, newly added paragraphs 15.1, 15.2 and 18.1. as well as the language added to paragraph 15 were not intended to alter the effect of the provision but should be understood as clarifications.

[80] See Article 5, paragraph 5, sub-paragraph f).

[81] See paragraph 76 of the Commentary to the Model Agreement.

[82] See Article 26, paragraph 3, sub-paragraphs c) of the Model Convention, Article 7, paragraph 4 of the Model Agreement and Article 21, paragraph 2, sub-paragraph (d) of the Council of Europe/OECD Convention.

[83] The previous version of the Commentary on Article 26 elaborated only briefly on the meaning of the term "public policy/ordre public." However, the more extensive

Model Agreement (paragraph 91) elaborate on the meaning of the term. "Public policy" generally refers to the vital interests of a country, for instance where information requested relates to a state secret. A case of "public policy" may also arise, for example, where a tax investigation in another country was motivated by racial or political persecution. Thus, this limitation rarely arises in practice.

13.4 Trade, business and other secrets

41. Both Article 26 of the Model Convention and Article 7 of the Model Agreement make clear that there is no obligation to supply information which would disclose any trade, business, industrial, commercial or professional secret or trade process.[84] The respective commentaries explain that these secrets should not be interpreted in too wide a sense. In particular, financial information, including books and records, does not by its nature constitute a trade, business or other secret. In the rare cases where the issue of a trade, business or other secret arises, the decision of whether or not to provide such information is left to the discretion of the requested State. Where in a particular case a contracting party decides to decline to provide certain information on such grounds it should excise the details of the trade, business or other secret from the relevant documentation and provide the remaining information to the other contracting party.[85] The role of the competent authority is to determine whether or not to pass on sensitive information and the local authorities that gather the information in the first instance should point out what might be sensitive. Ordinary tax secrecy protects trade and business secrecy in all countries. But in general neither the taxpayer nor a third party has a right to refuse to give such information to its tax administration.

discussion in the current version is intended to clarify rather than alter the meaning of the term.

84 In connection with the Council of Europe/OECD Convention see Article 21, paragraph 2, sub-paragraph (d).

85 For further details on trade, business or other secrets see paragraphs 78 through 83 of Commentary on the Model Agreement and paragraphs 19 through 19.2 of the Commentary on Article 26 Model Convention. The previous version of the Commentary on Article 26 did not elaborate on the meaning of the terms "trade, business, industrial, commercial or professional secret or trade process." However, the new language in the current version is intended to illustrate and explain the terms, not to alter their meaning.

Example: In responding to a request from country B, the competent authority of country A engages in a comprehensive investigation of pharmaceutical company C, resident in country A. As a result, the competent authority of country A is exposed to highly valuable commercial information concerning the manufacture of the product itself. Such information would be subject to the limitations described above and the competent authority of Country A could refuse to supply the information to country B, or at least excise that part of the information from the response to country B.

13.5 Legal professional privilege

42. A contracting party may decline to provide information in cases where the information constitutes a confidential communication between a client and an attorney, solicitor or other admitted legal representative. However, the rules on what constitutes a confidential communication should not be interpreted or applied in such a broad way so as to hamper effective exchange of information. In particular, no privilege should attach to documents or records delivered to an attorney, solicitor or other admitted legal representative in an attempt to protect such documents or records from disclosure.[86] In addition, a requested party would be expected to verify, and challenge if necessary, on behalf of the requesting party, the validity of a claim for legal professional privilege if such validity was in dispute.

13.6 Bank secrecy

43. In most countries, banks and similar financial institutions are required to protect the confidentiality of the financial affairs of their clients. This obligation ("bank secrecy") may not only protect bank information against disclosure to third parties but may also affect the access to such information by governmental authorities, including tax authorities. The practices of OECD member countries in this regard are summarised in the Report "Improving Access to Bank Information for Tax Purposes"(OECD, 2000) and in an update report issued in 2003 (the "2003 Progress Report").

---

86 For further details on legal professional privilege see paragraphs 19.3 and 19.4 on Article 26 of the Model Convention and Article 7, paragraph 3 of the Model Agreement plus the accompanying commentary (paragraphs 84 through 90). The previous version of the Commentary on Article 26 did not discuss the attorney – client privilege or similar privileges. However, the new language included in the current version only illustrates and explains these concepts without affecting the substantive rules regarding the limitations on the obligation to exchange information.

44. Both the Model Convention and the Model Agreement stipulate that bank secrecy can not form the basis for declining to provide information.[87] Thus, the competent authorities of the contracting parties need to have the authority to access, either directly or indirectly, through a judicial or administrative process, information held by banks or other financial institutions and to provide such information to the other contracting party. The respective commentaries elaborate further on this point. [88]

13.7 Information held by nominees, agents, fiduciaries and ownership information

45. A request for information cannot be declined solely because the information is held by nominees or persons acting in an agency or fiduciary capacity or because the information relates to an ownership interest.[89] For instance, an information request could not be declined merely because domestic law or practices may treat ownership information as a trade or business secret. The commentaries elaborate further on this point. [90]

Example 1: During a tax investigation, A, a resident of Country Y, claims that payments he made to B, a resident of Country Z, were in relation to services

---

[87] See Article 5, paragraph 4 Model Agreement and Article 26, paragraph 5 Model Convention. Paragraph 5 was added in the current version of Article 26 and no equivalent provision existed in the previous version. However, the Commentary on Article 26 explains that the addition of paragraph 5 should not be interpreted as suggesting that the previous version of Article 26 did not authorise the exchange of bank information and goes on to say that the vast majority of OECD member countries already exchanged bank information under the previous version of Article 26. See paragraph 19.10 of the Commentary on Article 26. Note that Austria, Belgium, Luxembourg and Switzerland have entered a reservation regarding paragraph 5.

[88] See paragraphs 19.10 through 19.15 of the Commentary on Article 26 of the Model Convention and paragraphs 46 through 48 of the Commentary on Article 5 of the Model Agreement. For details on any country specific procedural and other rules relating to access to bank information in OECD countries please see the Module on country profiles. Several countries have specific rules in this regard.

[89] See Article 5, paragraph 4 Model Agreement and Article 26, paragraph 5 Model Convention. Paragraph 5 was added in the current version of Article 26 and no equivalent provision existed in the previous version. For further details see footnote 32.

[90] See paragraphs 46 et seq. of the commentary on the Model Agreement and see paragraphs 19.12 through 19.15 of the Commentary on Article 26 of the Model Convention.

provided by another individual, C, whose identity and place of residence is unknown to A. The competent authority of Country Y believes C may be resident in Country Y and asked the competent authority of Country Z to obtain information concerning the identity of C from B, notwithstanding that B appears to have been acting in an agency/fiduciary capacity.

Example 2: An investigation by the tax authorities in Country Y, in relation to Company A, revealed payment of royalties to Company B which is resident in Country Z. Believing that the payments may be for the ultimate benefit of individual C, a resident of Country Y, the competent authority of Country Y approaches the competent authority of Country Z to obtain information about the company and the payment it received. Company B claims that the individual who controls the company was an ex-employee of Company A and if his identity is revealed this could lead to the commencement of a civil action against that individual. Notwithstanding the protestations of the company, the competent authority could not decline the request for details of the ownership of Company B.

13.8 Domestic tax interest

46. The concept of "domestic tax interest" describes a situation where a contracting party can only provide information to another contracting party if it has an interest in the requested information for its own tax purposes. A refusal to provide information can not be based on a domestic tax interest requirement and a contracting party must use its information gathering measures even though invoked solely to obtain and provide information to the other contracting party.[91] As stated in the 2003 Progress Report, there is no longer any OECD country that requires a domestic tax interest.

[91] Article 26, paragraph 4 Model Convention; Article 5(2) Model Agreement. Paragraph 4 was added in the current version of Article 26 to deal explicitly with the obligation to exchange information in situations where the requested information is not needed by the requested State for domestic tax purposes. In the previous version this obligation was not expressly stated in the Article, but was reflected in the Commentary. Paragraph 16 of the Commentary on Article 26 provided that this obligation was clearly evidenced by the practices followed by Member countries which showed that, when collecting information requested by a treaty partner, contracting states often use the special examining or investigative powers provided by their laws for purposes of levying their domestic taxes even though they do not themselves need the information for these purposes. Thus, the addition of new paragraph 4 should be seen as a clarification.

13.9 Request in conformity with the terms of the instrument pursuant to which it is made

47. The Model Agreement provides explicitly that a contracting party may decline to provide information where the request is not made in conformity with the Agreement.[92] For instance, Article 5(5) of the Model Agreement requires that in connection with a request the requesting Party must provide certain information to the competent authority of the requested Party. A failure to supply such information allows the requested Party to decline the request because the request is not made "in conformity with the Agreement." The Model Convention is less formalistic in this regard and leaves more leeway to the competent authorities but the basic principle applies equally. For instance, where a requesting party does not demonstrate the relevance of the requested information to an ongoing examination or enquiry, the requested party may decline the request because it does not meet the "forseeably relevant" standard and is thus outside the scope of Article 26. Of course, before declining a request on this basis the requested party should seek clarification from the other competent authority on this point.

13.10 Non-discrimination

48. A competent authority may refuse to supply information in cases involving discrimination of a national of the requested Party. This rule is contained in Article 7, paragraph 6 of the Model Agreement. In the context of the Model Convention the rule flows from the first sentence of Article 26 paragraph 1 ("… insofar as the taxation thereunder is not contrary to the Convention.") read in conjunction with Article 24, paragraph 1. This issue should only arise in exceptional circumstances and, thus, should be of little practical relevance. [93]

13.11 No obligation to carry out measures at variance with domestic laws and practices

49. The Model Convention provides that a Contracting State is not obligated to carry out administrative measures at variance with its law and administrative practice.[94] The underlying rationale is that a contracting party

[92] See Article 7, paragraph 1

[93] In connection with the Council of Europe/OECD Convention see Article 21, paragraph 2, sub-paragraph (f).

[94] Article 26, paragraph 3, sub-paragraph a) Model Convention. Previously, Article 26, paragraph 2, sub-paragraph a). In connection with the Council of Europe/OECD Convention, see Article 21, paragraph 2, sub-paragraph (c).

should be required to do no more -- but also no less – than it would if its own taxation was at stake. Thus, where the information in possession of the competent authority is not sufficient to reply to a request, a contracting party must take all relevant information gathering measures, including special investigations or special examinations of the business accounts, provided it would take similar measures for its own tax purposes.

50. The Model Agreement contains a similar rule[95] and provides that where the information in the possession of the competent authority is not sufficient to reply to a request, the requested party should take all relevant information gathering measures to provide the information requested. An information gathering measure is "relevant" if it is capable of obtaining the information requested. The decision to determine in a particular case which information gathering measures are relevant lies with the requested party.[96]

13.12 No obligation to provide information not obtainable under domestic law in the normal course of administration

51. Article 26, paragraph 3, sub-paragraph b) of the Model Convention provides that a Contracting State is free to decline to provide information if the information can not be obtained under its domestic law or can not be obtained in the normal course of administration. The Model Agreement does not contain a provision similar to Article 26.[97] However, both provide that

[95] Article 5, paragraph 2.

[96] The Model Convention and the Model Agreement use different approaches to reach a similar result. The Model Convention is built on the assumption that both contracting parties have a tax system and that therefore they should use the same types of information gathering measures irrespective of whether a matter relates to their taxation or to the taxation of a treaty partner. The Model Agreement, however, was developed in a context where one contracting party may not have any system of direct taxation. Such a country may then not have any tax related domestic information gathering measures and the "reciprocity approach" used in the Model Convention could not be applied. The Model Agreement therefore simply refers to all relevant information gathering measures.

[97] As already mentioned in the preceding footnote, the Model Convention uses a "reciprocity approach" which assumes that both countries have direct tax systems. This assumption is not valid in connection with the Model Agreement which was developed to permit use also for situations where one of its parties does not have a direct tax system. In this case the "reciprocity approach" can not be applied because a country without a direct tax system would have no "normal course of [tax]

irrespective of domestic law or domestic administrative practice a contracting Party cannot use bank secrecy or a domestic tax interest requirement as a basis for declining to provide information.[98] Furthermore, a request can not be declined because the information is held by a nominee or a person acting in an agency or fiduciary capacity or because it relates to an ownership interest.[99] Thus, the outcomes under the Model Convention and the Model Agreement are therefore largely the same.

14. Information Gathering Measures

52. The information requested may already be at the disposal of the tax administration of the requested party or it may require special information gathering measures. Which particular information gathering measure(s) is(are) most appropriate in an individual case will depend on all relevant facts and circumstances. Information gathering measures could include the following types of measures, provided, of course, that those measures are in line with the laws and administrative practice of the requested party:

- Question a person that may have knowledge of information or may be in possession, custody or control of information.

- Where voluntary co-operation can not be obtained, require a person to appear at a specified time and place for the taking of testimony.

- Where the person does not appear at the specified time and place take appropriate measures to compel such person's appearance.

- Request the production of books, papers, records or other tangible property.

- Question the individual producing books, papers, records or other tangible property regarding the purposes for which and the manner in which the item is or was maintained.

- Place the individual giving testimony or producing books, papers or other tangible property under oath.

administration" and no information may be "obtainable" for domestic tax purposes where a country imposes no tax.

[98] See Article 26, paragraphs 4 and 5 Model Convention and Article 5 paragraphs 2 and 4 Model Agreement.

[99] See Article 26, paragraph 5 Model Convention and Article 5(4)(b) Model Agreement.

– Gain access to and search premises for the purpose of locating and securing books and records or other tangible property for examination.

– Produce true and correct copies of books, papers, records or other tangible property.

– Permit the competent authority of the requesting State to provide written questions to which the individual giving testimony or producing books, papers, records or other tangible property is requested to respond.

15. Procedural Rights and Safeguards

53. Domestic laws provide for a variety of procedural rights and safeguards for persons affected by information gathering measures or more generally by information exchange. Such rights and safeguards include notification rules, a right to challenge the exchange of information following notification or rights to challenge information gathering measures taken by the requested party.

54. Several OECD member countries must notify the taxpayer subject to the enquiry and/or the person that provided the information in certain circumstances. This may result for the person notified in a mere right to be informed about the exchange, a right to be consulted or even a right to challenge the exchange. Some countries lift these notification requirements in cases of tax fraud or postpone notification until after the exchange. In some cases the obligation to notify is lifted if a federal court determines that notification would seriously jeopardise the investigation. Competent authorities should therefore indicate if there is suspicion of fraud in their requests if they wish to prevent the notification. In countries that require notification, taxpayers generally have the right to appeal the exchange of information. Notification rights no longer apply in VAT cases of exchange between member states of the European Union.[100]

55. Given the possible implications of such rights and safeguards for information exchange, contracting parties should inform each other of their legislation or administrative practice concerning notification (and any other procedural rights and safeguards that may be of relevance) when a tax information exchange agreement or an income tax convention is concluded and thereafter whenever the relevant rules are modified.[101]

16. Confidentiality of information received

[100] For more details see the Module on Country Profiles.

[101] See also paragraph 14.1 of the Commentary on Article 26 of the Model Convention.

56. Any information received should be treated as confidential.[102] The Model Agreement provides that the information received may be disclosed only to persons or authorities (including courts and administrative bodies) concerned with the assessment, collection and enforcement of the taxes covered by the Agreement (including the prosecution or the determination of appeals) and the information may be used only for such purposes. Information may not be disclosed to any other person or third jurisdiction without the express written consent of the competent authority of the requested party.

57. With respect to the disclosure rules, the Model Convention differs from the Model Agreement in several respects. First, the Model Convention also permits disclosure to oversight authorities.[103] Oversight authorities are authorities that supervise the tax administration and enforcement authorities as part of the general administration of the government of the contracting parties.[104] Second, the Model Convention does not permit disclosure to any other person, entity, authority or jurisdiction whereas the Model Agreement permits such disclosure provided express written consent is given by the competent authority of the requested party. Finally, while both the Model Agreement and the Model Convention require that information be kept confidential and then names the persons to whom the information can be disclosed, the Model Convention contains the additional requirement that information should be treated "as secret in the same manner as information obtained under domestic law."[105] However, because both the Agreement and the Convention specify to whom the information can be disclosed (thus ensuring a minimum standard of confidentiality), there should be little practical difference between the two formulations.

58. Under the rules of some countries, special procedural rules may apply to sensitive information. For instance, in connection with the provision of bank information Hungary requires that the requesting competent authority

---

102 See Article 26 paragraph 2 Model Convention, Article 8 Model Agreement, Article 22 of the Council of Europe/OECD Convention.

103 This is a change from the previous version of Article 26. Under the previous version of Article 26 information could not be disclosed to oversight authorities.

104 See paragraphs 12 and 12.1. of the Commentary on Article 26 of the Model Convention.

105 Again it needs to be borne in mind that the Model Agreement was developed for use also in situations where one of the parties has no direct tax system. Where a country has no tax system it is unlikely to have domestic rules on tax secrecy and the reference would then be meaningless.

signs a statement confirming the confidential treatment of the information provided by Hungary.

59. The confidentiality rules apply to all types of information, including both information provided in a request and information transmitted in response to a request. If the secrecy provisions under the domestic laws of a Contracting State are narrower than under the Model Agreement or the Model Convention, then the provisions of the Model Agreement or the Model Convention will have no consequences. If the domestic rules are broader, however, then the confidentiality provisions will put a restriction on the use of information received from abroad. The local tax authorities are under the obligation to refer to their competent authorities any issue which may arise concerning the disclosure of the information received.

60. Information received may also be communicated to the taxpayer his proxy or to a witness. However, while such disclosure is permitted, it is not required. In fact, the disclosure to the taxpayer or his proxy may raise an issue in certain cases, for instance where the information is given in confidence and the source of the information may have a legitimate interest in not disclosing it to the taxpayer. Similarly, the competent authorities may wish to keep confidential their correspondence with respect to any information exchanged. The competent authority supplying information should therefore indicate whether there are any objections to the disclosure of any part of the information provided (including any related correspondence) to the taxpayer, his proxy or to a witness. Where necessary the competent authorities should then discuss such issues with a view to finding a mutually acceptable solution.

61. Since information may be disclosed to the taxpayer or his proxy it may also be disclosed to any governmental or judicial authorities charged with deciding whether information should be released to the taxpayer.[106] This case may arise in countries where a taxpayer who has been denied access to his files by the tax authorities has the right to apply for a review of that decision by a review or appeals body. Logically, this body has to see the information in order to render its decision.

62. Many countries have domestic information disclosure laws such as freedom of information or other legislation that allows access to governmental documents and records. The confidentiality provisions in exchange of information instruments are intended to take precedence over any domestic rules that permit disclosure to persons not referred to in the

[106] See paragraph 12 of the Commentary on Article 26 Model Convention. The previous version of the commentary on Article 26 did not include such a clarification. However, no change in substance was intended.

confidentiality provision.[107] Any country which could not adhere to that principle and which is engaged in treaty negotiations should bring this point to the attention of the other contracting party. Where this issue arises as a result of a court decision or a subsequent change in legislation the competent authorities should inform other competent authorities at the earliest opportunity. It should be noted that confidentiality provisions of income tax conventions create obligations under international law. Any person faced with a request to release information supplied under an income tax convention or a tax information exchange agreement should consult with his or her competent authority, who may also inform the competent authority who supplied the information.

17. Use of information for other purposes

63. The information exchanged may not be used for purposes other than those for which it has been exchanged. Thus, the information pursuant to the Model Convention or the Model Agreement cannot be used for non-tax purposes. For instance, fiscal information obtained pursuant to the Model Convention or the Model Agreement must not be used for the prosecution of non-fiscal crimes. If the information appears to be of value to the receiving party for another purpose, it must resort to means specifically designed for that purpose, for example a judicial assistance treaty. When in doubt about whether information supplied by a foreign competent authority can be used for a purpose other than the tax purpose covered by the instrument under which it was provided, local authorities should always consult the competent authority.

64. Some countries, however, require the sharing of tax information by tax authorities with other law enforcement authorities and judicial authorities on matters such as money laundering, corruption or terrorism financing. As a result these countries may wish to include specific wording in their bilateral treaties to permit the sharing of information received pursuant to a tax information exchange agreement with such other authorities. The Commentary to the Model Convention provides language that can be used for this purpose.[108]

18. Cost of information exchange

[107] Paragraph 12 of the Commentary on Article 26 of the Model Convention expressly clarifies this point.

[108] See paragraph 12.3. of the Commentary on Article 26 of the Model Convention. Also note that similar language is contained in Article 22, paragraph 4 of the Council of Europe/OECD Convention.

65. The question of cost is addressed explicitly in Article 13 of the Model Agreement. The accompanying commentary (see paragraphs 98 and 99) elaborates on methods and approaches contracting parties may use in allocating costs related to information exchange. In practice, several tax information exchange agreements draw a distinction between ordinary and extraordinary costs. They then assign the responsibility to assume ordinary costs to the requested party but require the requesting party to bear any extraordinary costs.[109] "Extraordinary costs" are meant to cover, for instance, costs incurred when a particular form of procedure has been used at the request of the applicant party, costs incurred by third parties from which the requested party has obtained the information (for example bank information), or supplementary costs of experts, interpreters, or translators if needed, for example for elucidating the case or translating accompanying documents or damages which the requested party has been obliged to pay to the taxpayer as a result of measures taken on the request of the applicant party. Other tax information exchange agreements draw a distinction between direct and indirect costs and require the requesting party to bear all direct costs.

66. The Model Convention does not contain a provision on costs and any issue arising in connection with costs should therefore be discussed by the competent authorities. As a practical matter where costs turn out to be extraordinarily high countries seem prepared to find practical solutions. There are examples where the requesting party has offered to bear the cost of translation and certification of copies or has put manpower and equipment at the disposal of the treaty partner to reduce the burden of the requested party. In these cases it might also be worth considering whether – provided this is permitted under domestic law – the presence of foreign tax officials as part of a "tax examination abroad" could be used to reduce the cost on the requested party. In any event it is important that this issue is addressed at an early stage to allow for a timely and cost efficient solution.

19. Use of Taxpayer Identification Numbers (TINs)

67. Most OECD member countries attribute Tax Identification Numbers (TINs) to their resident taxpayers and some countries also assign TINs to non-residents under certain circumstances. In 1997 the OECD Council adopted a Recommendation on the use of TINs in the international context (C(1997)39/FINAL). TINs are used to identify taxpayers and are a key to automated matching programs. The knowledge of TINs can be useful for processing information received automatically from a treaty partner. The

[109] This approach is also found in Article 26 of the Council of Europe/OECD Convention.

provision of TINs is also important when either making or answering a request or providing information spontaneously since it will facilitate the quick identification of the taxpayer. Consequently when the provision of TINs is legally possible field tax officials should provide them to their competent authority when making a request or transmitting information (both source country and residence country TINs, if known).

The 2006 OECD Manual on Information Exchange – Module 1 on Exchange of Information on Request

1. Exchange of information on request describes a situation where one competent authority asks for particular information from another competent authority. Typically, the information requested relates to an examination, inquiry or investigation of a taxpayer's tax liability for specified tax years. Information exchange upon request can be divided into several stages or steps and this section provides guidance on each of these steps:

- Step 1: Preparing and sending a request
- Step 2: Receiving and checking a request
- Step 3: Gathering the requested information
- Step 4: Replying to the request
- Step 5: Providing feedback

STEP 1: PREPARING AND SENDING A REQUEST

Preliminary considerations

2. Before sending a request, a contracting party should use all means available in its own territory to obtain the information except where those would give rise to disproportionate difficulties. The efforts by the requesting party should also include attempts to obtain information in the other contracting party before making a request, for example by use of the internet, and where practical, commercial databases or engaging diplomatic staff located in that country to obtain publicly available information. The OECD has developed a reference

guide on sources of information abroad to assist competent authorities in identifying the types of information available in other countries (See *www.oecd.org/taxation*).

Form of the request

3. The request by the competent authority should be made in writing but in urgent cases an oral request may be accepted, where permitted under the applicable laws and procedures, for the purposes of initiating an enquiry on the condition that it is followed up by written confirmation. In response to demand from its member countries for a fast and secure method for exchanging information electronically, the OECD has developed a procedure for transmitting confidential information using encrypted attachments to email messages.

Content of the request

4. Drafting the request in a complete and comprehensive manner is very important. The competent authority should put himself in the position of the recipient of the request and include the information in the request that he would consider important if he were receiving the request. The request should be as detailed as possible and contain all the relevant facts, so that the competent authority that receives the request is well aware of the needs of the applicant contracting party and can deal with the request in the most efficient manner. An incomplete request will increase delays since the foreign competent authority may have to ask for more details to answer the request properly. Also note that certain countries have established checklists of information necessary to carry out certain procedures for obtaining information For details please see the module on country profiles.

5. While every case may differ on the particular facts and circumstances, the following **checklist of what to include in a request** seeks to provide some guidance on what could be included in a request. Note that responding to a request should not be delayed by endeavouring to obtain every item on the checklist, abbreviations should not be used and other relevant information may be added.

1. The reference to the legal basis upon which the request is based.

2. A statement confirming that your tax administration has pursued all means available in its own territory to obtain the information except those that would give rise to disproportionate difficulties.

3. A statement that the request is in conformity with the laws and administrative practices of your country, that your tax administration could obtain the information if it was within your country and that the request is in conformity with the legal instrument on which it is based.

4. The identity of the person(s) under examination or investigation: name, date of birth (for individuals), marital status (if relevant), TIN and address (including email or internet addresses, if known).

5. The identity of any foreign taxpayer(s) or entity(ies) relevant to the examination or investigation and, to the extent known, their relationship to the person(s) under examination or investigation: name, marital status (if relevant),TIN (if known), addresses (including email or internet addresses if known), registration number in the case of a legal entity (if known), charts, diagrams or other documents illustrating the relationships between the persons involved.

6. If the information requested involves a payment or transaction via an intermediary mention the name, addresses and TIN (if known) of the intermediary, including, if known, the name and address of the bank branch as well as the bank account number when bank information is requested.

7. Relevant background information including the tax purpose for which the information is sought, the origin of the enquiry, the reasons for the request and the grounds for believing that the information requested is held in the territory of the requested party or is in the possession or control of a person within the jurisdiction of the requested party.

8. The stage of the procedure in the requesting party, the issues identified and whether the investigation is of a civil or administrative nature only or may also have criminal consequences. Where references are made to domestic law it is useful to provide some explanation as the foreign competent authority will not be familiar with your laws.

9. The information requested and why it is needed. Also specify the information that may be pertinent (*e.g.* invoices, contracts).

10. In the context of an income tax convention, whether the request relates to the application of a tax convention or the administration or enforcement of domestic legislation.

11. The taxes concerned, the tax periods under examination (day, month, year they begin and end), and the tax periods for which information is requested (if they differ from the years examined give the reasons why).

12. The currency concerned whenever figures are mentioned.

13. The urgency of the reply. State the reasons for the urgency and, if applicable, indicate the date after which the information may no longer be useful.

14. Whether a translation should be provided if possible (in urgent cases mentioning that no translation is required could speed up the exchange).

15. If copies of documents or bank records are requested, what type of authentication is necessary, if any.

16. If the information is likely to be used in a court proceeding and the applicable rules of evidence require the information to be in a certain form, the form should be indicated to the other competent authority.

17. Whether there are reasons for avoiding notification of the taxpayer under examination or investigation (*e.g.* if notification may endanger the investigation).

18. The name, phone, fax number and e-mail address of the tax official who may be contacted if needed, if that person is a delegate of the competent authority.

6. The statements mentioned in # 2 and 3 are mandatory in connection with information exchange based on the Model Agreement. In the case of information exchange based on Article 26 they are optional and whether they should be included in the request will depend on the particular circumstances. Regarding reciprocity, see also the discussion in the section on General and Legal Aspects of Exchange of Information.

Language

7. The request by the competent authority should be drafted in a simple and clear manner. It should be prepared in the native language of the requesting party and accompanied, where practicable, with a translation into the language of the requested party or a common third language. Alternatively, where this facilitates effective exchange of information, the request may be drafted only in the language of the requested party or a common third language. Any translation should be

left to the competent authority of the requesting party if the foreign language skills are not sufficient at the local level.

8. When responding to a request for information, special problems may arise in the translation of attached documents such as agreements, business correspondence, invoices etc. If no translation is provided by the requested party, the relevant elements of the attached documents should, where practicable, be identified by the requested party so that the requesting party does not take unnecessary time translating information which may be irrelevant to the request.

Procedure

9. The request should be forwarded by the tax examiner to his competent authority through the normal official channels. The competent authority will verify that the request meets all the necessary requirements and then transmit the request to his counterpart in the foreign country.

Impact of requests for information on the statute of limitations

10. In certain countries (*e.g.* France) the sending of a request for information concerning a case subject to a tax examination will suspend the statute of limitations. Tax examiners should refer to their domestic rules on this point.

STEP 2: RECEIVING AND CHECKING A REQUEST

11. A competent authority should acknowledge receipt of a request as soon as possible. The competent authority will then check whether or not the request is valid and complete, *i.e.* confirm that:

- it fulfils the conditions set forth in the applicable exchange of information provision;
- it has been signed by the competent authority and includes all the necessary information to process the request;
- the information requested is of a nature which can be provided having regard to the legal instrument on which it is based and the relevant laws of the requested party;
- sufficient information is provided to identify the taxpayer; and

– sufficient information is given to understand the request.

12. In the process of reviewing whether the request is valid and complete, the competent authority will also consider whether there are grounds for declining the request (see the discussion on "limitations to exchange of information" in the section on General and Legal Aspects of Exchange of Information). Note also that such grounds may also emerge later in the process (*e.g.* an attempt to obtain the information may be resisted based on the assertion that the information is protected by the attorney client privilege) and will then have to be considered at that stage.

13. If the competent authority concludes that the request is invalid or incomplete it should notify the applicant party of any deficiencies in the request as soon as possible. If it is valid and complete the receiving competent authority will seek to gather the information itself or pass the request on to officials with the necessary investigative and information gathering powers. In some countries the competent authority instructs a local tax office to gather the information and may also impose a deadline within which to report back.

14. The competent authority may invite a representative of its counterpart to come and clarify the request or to attend the interview of the taxpayer or even to be present in a tax examination. This may be a useful option for reducing costs and resource commitments for the requested party. For further information please consult the module on tax examinations abroad.

Request received directly from foreign local tax official

15. The unauthorised exchange of information can jeopardise the success of an investigation or prosecution. Local tax officials are not entitled to exchange information directly with their foreign counterparts unless they have received a delegation of powers from their competent authority and an authorization from the foreign competent authority. It may happen that a tax official receives a request which has bypassed his or both competent authorities. In such a case, the tax official should immediately pass it on to his competent authority and the answer should go through the appropriate competent authorities. It may decide to reject the request or to ask its counterpart whether the request is worth processing. If it is the case, the foreign competent authority will produce a new request according to the normal procedure but the tax official should not wait to start gathering the information. See also the general discussion of this point in the section on General and Legal Aspects of Exchange of Information.

STEP 3: GATHERING INFORMATION

16. Gathering information for another country should be given a high priority because exchange of information is mandatory and a prompt and comprehensive reply is likely to contribute to the same type of treatment in a reverse situation. If the information is not available, the other contracting party should be informed as soon as possible via the competent authority.

17. In most countries, the governing principle is that the information is to be gathered as if it were sought for domestic tax purposes. Information requested may be of two types:

- information which is already at the disposal of the tax administration (tax return, income declared, expenses claimed, etc.); or

- information obtainable by the competent authority but requiring a more time consuming approach. For example, it may be necessary to interview a taxpayer, to undertake a tax investigation, or to obtain information from a third party such as a bank. Additional information which is likely to be useful to the requesting country should also be included in the response, even if it is not specifically requested.

18. As a time-saving measure, a translation of the reply in the language of the requesting party could be prepared if there are language skills at the local or competent authority level. If documents such as contracts are enclosed and cannot be translated the relevant parts of those documents should be identified. Efforts should also be made to pass on the information in a format which meets the requesting party's evidentiary or other legal requirement if so requested (and to the extent allowable under domestic law), *e.g.* provide authenticated copies of original records.

STEP 4: REPLYING TO A REQUEST

19. Based on the information that has been gathered the competent authorities will prepare the reply to the information request. In certain countries the reply may also be prepared by a local tax office

and the competent authority will then only review the reply. If prescribed under domestic law, and provided no exceptions apply, the competent authority will then notify the taxpayer. If no notification is required the information will be passed on to the foreign competent authorities with a mention as to the limits on the use of the information. If the information touches upon trade and business secrets, the competent authority may wish to get in touch with the other competent authority in order to establish how the information is to be used and what protective measures that State has according to its internal provisions to protect such secrets.

Checklist of what to include in the response

20. While every case may differ on the particular facts and circumstances, the following checklist of what to include in a request seeks to provide some guidance on what could be included in a request. Note that exchanges should not be delayed by endeavouring to obtain every item on the checklist and that abbreviations should not be used.

1. The reference to the legal basis pursuant to which the information is provided.

2. A reference to the request in response to which the information is provided.

3. The information requested, including copies of documents (*e.g.* records, contracts, invoices) as well as any information not specifically requested but likely to be useful based on the information provided in connection with the request. Where reference is made to domestic laws an explanation should be added as the foreign competent authority will not be familiar with these rules.

4. If applicable, explanation why certain information could not be provided or could not be provided in the form requested. Note that the inability to provide the information in the form requested does not affect the obligation to provide the information.

5. For money amounts indicate currency, whether a tax has been withheld and if so the rate and amount of tax.

6. The type of action taken to gather the information.

7. The tax periods for which the information is provided.

8. Mention whether the taxpayer or a third person has been notified about the exchange.

9. Mention whether there are any objections to notifying the taxpayer of the receipt of the information.

10. Mention whether there are any objections to disclosing all or certain parts of the information provided to the taxpayer (*e.g.* the transmittal letter).

11. Mention whether feedback is requested on the usefulness of the information.

12. A reminder that the use of the information provided is subject to the applicable confidentiality rules (*e.g.* by stamping a reference to the applicable confidentiality rule on the information provided).

13. The name, phone, fax number and e-mail address of the tax official who may be contacted if needed, if that person is a delegate of the competent authority.

Standard time objectives

21. The time required to obtain tax information depends on whether the information is available in the tax files or whether an investigation and/or contact with third parties is necessary. Gathering the information through an investigation or via contact with third parties will naturally take more time. However, a competent authority should seek to provide the requested information within 90 days of receipt of a request. If the competent authority of the requested party is unable to provide the information within the 90 day period it should inform the other competent authority and explain the reasons for not having provided the information within the 90 day period (e.g. a necessary judicial procedure has not been completed). The underlying idea is that the requesting competent authority can expect to either receive the information within the 90 day period or at least to obtain a status report at the end of that period.[110]

STEP 5: PROVIDING FEEDBACK

22. Regular, timely and comprehensive feedback between competent authorities is important as it:

- enables quality improvements to be made for future information exchanges;

[110] See also Article 5, paragraph 6, sub-paragraph b) Model Agreement

- can improve the motivation of tax officials to provide information; and
- may be useful for competent authorities to obtain the resources they need as it will serve as an indicator of the usefulness of exchange.

23. Requesting competent authorities should, in appropriate cases, consider providing feedback to requested competent authorities regarding the usefulness of the information supplied. Feedback to the requested competent authority may include details of, for example, additional tax revenue raiscd, tax evasion methods detected and an overall assessment of how useful the information was to the tax administration. Requested competent authorities should subsequently consider providing any feedback received to their tax administration staff that were responsible for obtaining the requested information. For instance, where the staff of a local tax office invested significant time and effort in obtaining the requested information within a short time frame, a requesting competent authority may be well advised to provide feedback in order to motivate the local office staff to show the same dedication and commitment in connection with any future requests.

EXAMPLE OF REQUEST FOR INFORMATION

FROM	**TO**
Mr Competent Authority of Country X	Mr Competent Authority of Country Y
Director of Taxes	Director of Taxes
1234 Tax Boulevard	567 Free Street
Capital city 21001 Country X	Freedom City 34002 Country Y
phone/fax	

Reference CA/10 01 04 U

10.January, 2004

Taxpayer under investigation: PC Company
TIN: 89 67 89 02
56 A Street
Blueville 10001
Country X

Tax years under investigation:
01/10/00 - 30/09/01
01/10/01 - 30/09/02
01/10/02 - 30/09/03

Years for which information is requested: same years

Dear Mr. Competent Authority of Country Y

Re: request for information under Article 26 of the tax Convention between Country X and Country Y

This request is presented according to Article 26 of the tax convention between our two countries. Our request concerns PC Company above mentioned. The local tax office of Blueville is presently examining its income tax returns for the tax periods referred to above.

PC company is in the business of importing high tech equipment in the computer industry and selling this equipment to its domestic subsidiaries. During the tax examination it was discovered that funds have been deposited into a bank account (number: 001 678 543 at the State Bank , 1 Bank Street Freedom City 34001 Country Y. We believe the account is in the name of Mr John Smith TIN 57 06 2345 born 15 06 57 address 1 Blue Street, Blueville 10003 who owns 65% of the shares of PC Company and is the executive manager. We believe that the funds deposited into this account are taxable in Country X and have not been reported.

We therefore request the following information for the period under investigation:

Bank records including bank statements, concerning account n° 001 678 543 identified as being used directly or indirectly by PC Company or by Mr John Smith.

If you need more information please contact Mr Green phone: 1234567 fax 12344568. Would you acknowledge receipt of this request and indicate when the information is likely to be provided.

This request is presented according to Article 26 of our tax treaty and the information provided will be used only as provided for in such Article.

Sincerely,
Mr Competent Authority of Country X

EXAMPLE OF RESPONSE TO A REQUEST

FROM	TO
Mr. Competent Authority of Country Y Director of . 567 Free Street Freedom City 34002 Country Y Phone: Fax: Person to contact: Mr. Freed	Mr. Competent Authority of Country X Director of Taxes 1234 Tax Boulevard Capital City 21001 6 June 2004

Dear Mr. Competent Authority,

**Re: your request for information under Article 26 of the Tax Convention between Country X and
Country Y**

Your reference CA/1001 94 U
Taxpayer PC Company
TIN 89 67 89 02
56 A street
Blueville 10001

Tax Years for which information is requested:
01/10/00-30/09/01
01/10/01-30/09/02
01/10/02-30/09/03

On 10 January 2004, you presented a request for information under Article 26 of the Tax Convention between our two countries concerning bank accounts identified as being used directly or indirectly by PC Company or by Mr. John Smith the executive manager of PC Company.

Please find enclosed the bank records of the account number n(001 678 543). Our central file of bank accounts allowed us to identify another account opened on 5.08.92 by Mr. John Smith, City Bank n° 001 725 613, at the Branch located at 56 City Street in Freedom City.

This information is provided under Article 26 above-mentioned and its use is covered accordingly. Please provide information on the usefulness of the information supplied.

Yours sincerely,

Mr. Competent Authority of Country Y

Enclosures:
Bank Account State Bank n° 001 678 543
Copies of 36 bank statements
Bank Account City Bank n° 001 725 613
Copies of 17 bank statements

EXAMPLES OF INFORMATION EXCHANGE UPON REQUEST

The following examples seek to illustrate typical requests

Example 1: Inbound Loan

Taxpayer T, a resident of country A, pays interest on a loan made by company C, resident in country B. T claims not to be the beneficial owner of C. Tax auditors suspect that T is the beneficial owner of C and that the "loan" was actually an attempt to repatriate previously unreported income earned in country A. (*e.g.* because company C does not require any collateral or security for the loan or the credit conditions otherwise depart from what is typically agreed between unrelated parties).

The competent authority may request:

- Accounting records/financial statements of C for the relevant years;
- Relevant contracts and the related bank information evidencing the transfers, copies of signature cards on C's bank accounts;
- All documents indicating the source of the funds if the financial statements show that C did not have the necessary capital to make the loan;
- Information on the identity of the shareholders and/or beneficial owners in company C;
- Formation documents for C.

Example 2: Outbound Loan

Resident taxpayer T grants a loan to company C, resident in B. Unusual credit conditions lead to the suspicion, that T is related to C and that C has made a back to back loan to another person at normal credit conditions, thus shifting considerable profits to C.

The competent authority may request:

- Accounting records/ financial statements of C;
- Related contracts and bank statements on the receipt and on the use of the loan;
- Statement of dividend payments or other payments to shareholders of C;
- Information on shareholders in company C.

Example 3: Services Re-invoicing

Resident company A claims a deduction for services invoiced by company C, resident in foreign country B. However, the tax official auditing company A learns that the services were performed by resident taxpayer T. The income tax return of T only shows income from services provided to C and the amount invoiced by T to C is significantly smaller than the amount invoiced by C to A. The tax auditor suspects that C only acts as a re-invoicing agent because T's lifestyle far exceeds his declared income. The auditor suspects that C charges T only a small fee for its re-invoicing services and that the difference between the amount declared by T and the amount invoiced by C (minus its fee) is paid into a bank account held by T with a bank resident in B. (Note that in a variation of this structure T could also be purporting to be an employee of C and then only declare his wage income as taxable income).

The competent authority may request:

- Names and addresses of persons employed by C;
- Invoices of T to C and any payments made to him;
- All accounts payable of C with respect to T for the years under investigation;
- Accounting and financial records of C (in particular any bank records showing transfers by C to T).

Example 4: Import and export transaction using conduit companies

Resident company T purchases electronic components for use in its manufacturing operations from company C, resident in B. A tax inspector auditing company T becomes suspicious because the price charged by C to T far exceeds comparable prices in the industry. The tax inspector suspects that the amount invoiced is significantly higher than the amount C pays to the producer of the components. The tax inspector further suspects that in reality company C acts as an agent and that its likely paper profits are paid to a third party related to company T.

The competent authority may request:

- Information about direct imports/exports or the imports/exports via C (invoices of the forwarding agents, customs documents);
- Information about size and operation of C's premises and warehouses (*e.g.* copy of the lease showing size of premises and any rental payments due);
- Information about number of employees of C;
- Information about the persons acting for C, their remuneration, actual salary and social security payments;
- Accounting records/financial statements for C;
- If C claims to be an independent agent: information about the persons acting as agent, names and addresses, their remuneration, proof of the actual salary and social security payments made.

Based on the information provided by the competent authorities of country B the tax inspector is able to prove that company C deposited the difference between the purchase and the sales price (minus a small fee) into an account which A, the sole shareholder of T, has with a bank resident in B. A had not disclosed these payments in his income tax return.

The OECD's Project on Harmful Tax Practices Consolidated Application Note Guidance in Applying the 1998 Report to Preferential Tax Regimes

This section of the handbook contains an application note on Transparency and Effective Exchange of Information. The notes are an extract from a Consolidated Application Note which was developed to provide guidance to assist in the evaluation of preferential regimes in OECD member countries on a generic basis.

The guidance provided in the notes is intended to help countries assess whether a particular regime contains harmful elements.

The material on exchange of information is based on the same standard as the Global Forum uses in its work. With regard to transparency some elements described in the chapter will be familiar whereas other elements were developed for different purposes and may not have the same relevance to the Global Forum's work. Overall, it should be kept in mind that the chapter was written for the purposes of determining if a particular tax regime contained harmful elements and not whether a jurisdiction was able to cooperate fully in international tax matters.

The complete text of the application notes can be found at: *http://www.oecd.org/dataoecd/60/32/30901132.pdf*

TRANSPARENCY AND EXCHANGE OF INFORMATION

A. Introduction

14. This Chapter discusses the criteria of transparency and effective exchange of information. It focuses on particular transparency and exchange of information practices within the scope of the 1998 Report. Transparency and effective exchange of information are closely linked concepts because lack of transparency can prevent the effective exchange of information. This Chapter looks at both factors and, in particular, discusses the importance of:

- the existence of relevant and reliable information;
- the legal ability of a State to obtain information for the purposes of transmitting it to the State requesting the information;
- legal mechanisms permitting the exchange of information;
- adequate safeguards to protect the confidentiality of the information exchanged; and
- administrative measures to ensure that the exchange of information will function effectively.

15. Parts B and C of this Chapter provide guidance on transparency and effective exchange of information. Part D provides examples of the types of information that countries should be able to obtain and provide with respect to the particular types of preferential regimes identified in the 2000 Report.

16. The jurisdictions that have made commitments to co-operate with the OECD have made a substantial contribution in this field through their participation in the Global Forum Working Group on Effective Exchange of Information (the "Working Group"). The Working Group was established to develop a model legal instrument that could be used to establish effective exchange of information. Its work has informed the development of this Chapter and the instrument is in the Appendix to this document.

17. The transparency and information exchange practices described in this Chapter should not be viewed as undermining the legitimate role of bank secrecy in protecting the financial privacy of a bank's customer. See generally the 2000 OECD Report *"Improving Access to Bank Information for Tax Purposes."* Unauthorised disclosure of bank information could jeopardise the financial welfare of the clients of a bank or otherwise pose a threat to such clients. For this reason, as discussed further in this Chapter, access to bank information is to be provided only in the context of legitimate civil or

criminal tax investigations, and any information provided must be protected from inappropriate disclosure by strict confidentiality rules.

B. Transparency

18. Lack of transparency may arise in two broad contexts: (1) in the way in which a regime is designed and administered, including favourable application of laws and regulations, negotiable tax provisions, and a failure to make widely available administrative practices; and (2) the existence of provisions such as secrecy laws or inadequate ownership and other information requirements that prevent (or would prevent) effective exchange of information. The first point, including the specific exchange of information aspects, is also dealt with in the Chapters on rulings and transfer pricing, below.

19. Exchange of information can only be effective where it is combined with a regulatory framework that seeks to ensure that (1) relevant and reliable information exists and (2) the requested State has the ability to obtain the information for purposes of information exchange.

i) The existence of relevant and reliable information

20. If the information needed to respond to a request is not required by local law to be maintained for tax, regulatory or commercial reasons, or is not required to be retained for a reasonable period, it may not be available for exchange at the time a request is made for the information.

a) Books and records

21. Companies and other persons are generally required to keep books and records for tax, commercial, regulatory or other reasons. However, the value of books and records will depend on their reliability. Information is more likely to be reliable if there is some external check on the information. For example, if companies are required to keep books and records but there is no requirement to file a tax return based on those records, no obligation to file statements of account with a regulatory body, or no requirement for annual external audits, the company may have no incentive to keep accurate records in accordance with internationally accepted accounting practices. As a result, the information may be unreliable for purposes of applying the tax laws of a country requesting the information.

22. In the context of analysing record keeping requirements, rules about minimum retention periods for those books and records should also be assessed. In many business sectors, like the banking sector, regulators have established minimum record retention requirements for regulatory purposes.

For example, the Financial Action Task Force ("FATF") has addressed this issue in Recommendation 12 of its Forty Recommendations, which establishes a minimum retention period of five years for financial institutions. Similarly, in order to be able to substantiate information reported on tax returns, taxpayers generally must retain relevant information until the statute of limitations applicable to that tax year has expired.

b) Information on identity of legal and beneficial owners and other persons

23. Effective exchange requires the existence of information on companies, partnerships, trusts, foundations and other persons. If such information is not required to be kept for tax, regulatory, commercial or other reasons, it may not be available for exchange at the time an information request is received. The information should cover the type of information that other countries might legitimately expect to receive in response to a request. Information should be available on all persons that come within the territorial jurisdiction of a given country. Countries should ensure that such information is either maintained or obtainable by the authorities and can be exchanged upon request. [111]

24. In connection with companies and partnerships, countries should ensure that information is obtainable on the legal owners, who will very often also be the beneficial owners. A legal ownership interest in a partnership includes any form of interest, whether general or limited, capital or profit.

25. However, the availability of information concerning ownership should not stop with legal ownership. In some cases a legal ownership position may be subject to a nominee or similar arrangement. Where the legal owner acts on behalf of another person as a nominee or under a similar arrangement, such other person, rather than the legal owner, will often be the beneficial owner. An example of a nominee arrangement is a nominee shareholding arrangement where the legal title-holder that also appears as the shareholder of record acts as agent for another person. In these cases, and in other cases where the legal owner is not (or is just partly) the economic owner, information should be obtainable by the authorities on the economic owner(s) in addition to information on the legal owner(s). In this way, a treaty partner is able to apply its rules on beneficial ownership irrespective of

111. This Chapter does not address the mechanisms that may be used to obtain ownership information. The OECD Report "*Behind the Corporate Veil: Using Corporate Entities for Illicit Purposes*" (OECD 2001) sets forth a "menu" of different options for obtaining and sharing beneficial ownership and control information.

the precise juridical or economic interpretation of its beneficial ownership definition.

26. In connection with trusts and foundations, information should be obtainable on the identity of settlors, founders, trustees, members of a foundation council, beneficiaries and any other person who is in a position to direct how assets or revenue of the trust or foundation are to be dealt with. The term "foundation council" should be interpreted very broadly to include any person or body of persons managing the foundation or otherwise having the authority to act on behalf of the foundation. Information should also be obtainable with respect to persons that are substantially similar to trusts or foundations. However, it is recognised that where a trust, foundation or similar arrangement supports a general cause and does not have an identified group of persons as beneficiaries only limited information on beneficiaries may exist. Nevertheless even where such arrangements exist, information regarding the identity of persons directing the use of assets or distribution of revenue should be maintained or be obtainable. In addition, information on the persons benefiting from such uses and distributions should be maintained or be obtainable for the purposes of exchange of information.

27. Most organisational structures will be classified as a company, a partnership, a trust, a foundation or a person similar to a trust or foundation. However, there might be entities or structures for which information might be legitimately requested but that do not fall in any of these categories. For instance, an investment vehicle may be of a purely contractual nature. In these cases, information should be obtainable on any person with a right to share in the income or gain of the structure or in the proceeds from any sale or liquidation.

28. Ensuring the availability of updated ownership information, for information exchange purposes, might prove difficult with respect to publicly traded companies and collective investment funds where changes in ownership are very frequent. This Chapter therefore recognises that in these cases a more liberal standard can be applied. This standard is set out in detail in the model instrument developed by the Working Group (see Appendix) and applies equally for purposes of this Chapter.

c) Information on preferential regimes and their application to particular taxpayers

29. Some countries require an authorisation, license, ruling or similar administrative act for the application of a special regime. If the guidance provided in Chapter V on rulings does not apply to this type of regime and if the administration has discretionary powers to apply the special regime, the

decisions, additional conditions and underlying information should be maintained. Underlying information includes information provided by the taxpayer to qualify for the benefits of the regime.

30. Moreover, information on the application of a preferential regime to a particular taxpayer should be maintained. This information should include information on income as well as any deductions, provisions, depreciation, etc, which lower the taxable profit. In addition, information should be maintained on the rate on which the taxable income is taxed, which should include any reduction of the normal tax rate at which the taxable income is taxed. Information about the distribution of dividends and interest paid on shareholder loans should also exist. Information on the number of staff and qualification of staff of the entity including their employment contracts should be kept. As far as documentation in connection with regimes involving the selection or application of transfer pricing methods or that are implemented through rulings, the guidance in the Chapters on transfer pricing and rulings should be taken into account.

31. Countries should use the guidance set out in the box below to assess whether a preferential regime that meets the no or low tax criterion lacks transparency because relevant information is not maintained or is not obtainable.

The following features are likely to result in a lack of transparency:

1. The country's authorities, the persons concerned, or third parties subject to its jurisdiction do not maintain, or could not obtain information on:

- Ownership (both legal and beneficial) of companies, partnerships and other persons.
- Books and records of companies, partnerships and other persons.
- Trusts and foundations (*e.g.*, type, identity of settlors, trustees, members of foundation council, beneficiaries).
- The movement of assets.
- The identity of managers of collective investment funds.
- Ownership of bank accounts and transactional information.

- Reserves, insurance premiums paid and gains arising on life insurance in the case of insurance and re-insurance companies.
- Details of transactions with related parties.

2. A country has no requirement for filing tax returns, for filing financial accounts with a regulatory body or for external audits of accounts, and has no other adequate filing or auditing requirement that would ensure the reliability of books and records.

3. The tax, commercial or regulatory requirements do not ensure that books and records are retained for a reasonable period. A record retention period of five years or more would be considered a reasonable period.

4. The administration of a country has discretionary power to grant a preferential regime, but decisions, additional conditions and underlying information are not maintained by the authorities or by persons subject to its jurisdiction.

5. A person benefits from a preferential regime granted by a country but the information described in paragraphs 29 and 30 is not maintained by the authorities of such country or by persons subject to its jurisdiction.

ii) Access to the information

32. If the relevant information is kept, a tax or other appropriate authority should have the legal ability to obtain such information. Thus, tax authorities or other appropriate authorities should have adequate information gathering powers to be able to obtain information for purposes of information exchange. Such information gathering powers are, however, constrained by jurisdictional limitations. Thus, a requested State is not obligated to provide information which is neither held by its authorities nor is in the possession or control of persons who are within its territorial jurisdiction.

33. In the context of a request for information relating to a criminal tax matter, information should be obtainable without regard to whether the conduct being investigated would constitute a crime under the laws of the requested State if it occurred in the requested State.

34. In the context of a civil or criminal tax matter, the requested State should be able to obtain the information whether or not the requested State

has a need for the information for its own tax purposes. A requirement of a domestic tax interest could impede effective exchange of information, particularly where the requested State has no income tax. For instance, a preferential regime can imply that the profits are exempted from taxes. The country offering the exemption may determine that it does not need any information on a person benefiting from the regime for its own purposes. A similar determination may be made by a country that does not levy taxes on business profits. Nevertheless, the information may still be relevant to another country (*e.g.* the country of residence of the parent company).

35. Countries should use the guidance set out in the box below to assess whether a preferential regime that meets the no or low tax criterion lacks transparency because of the lack of access to information.

The following features are likely to result in a lack of transparency:

- A country cannot obtain and provide, in response to a specific request, information in criminal tax matters unless the conduct being investigated would constitute a crime under the laws of the requested country if it occurred there.
- A country cannot obtain and provide information in response to a specific request unless it also needs the information for its own tax purposes.
- A country cannot obtain and provide the information described in the box following paragraph 31 in response to a specific request.

C. Exchange of Information

36. Exchange of information requires a legal mechanism for providing the information to another State for tax administration purposes. Such legal mechanism should be coupled with adequate safeguards to protect the confidentiality of the information exchanged. Finally, there should be administrative measures to ensure that the exchange of information functions effectively.

i) Legal mechanisms for exchange of information

37. In general, information exchange occurs pursuant to a bilateral or multilateral treaty or an agreement that explicitly authorises the exchange of information for tax purposes. The model instrument developed by the

Working Group (see Appendix) provides an appropriate legal framework for exchange of information. Countries may choose whatever instruments they deem most appropriate to permit information exchange. The important point is not the use of a specific instrument but the existence of an effective mechanism for information exchange.

38. In order to have effective exchange with respect to preferential regimes that meet the low or no effective tax rate factor, the scope of the agreement should be broad so that the scope itself does not become an obstacle to exchange. For example, an agreement limited to exchange with respect to criminal matters only would result in very limited exchange. In some cases, it is difficult to determine without the information located in the foreign jurisdiction whether the acts committed by the taxpayer would constitute a criminal act or would be a lesser offence.

ii) Type of exchange of information

39. Exchange of information generally occurs in one of three different forms: upon request, spontaneous or automatic.[112] Effective exchange of information within the meaning of the 1998 Report does not require automatic exchange of information.

40. Effective exchange of information within the meaning of the 1998 Report is limited to information exchange upon request except in the situations described in the Chapters on transfer pricing and rulings. Information exchange upon request does not cover mere "fishing expeditions".

iii) Limitations on exchange of information

41. Although a broad scope is encouraged, it is recognised in all treaties and agreements for exchange of information that there may be circumstances where it may be inappropriate to require the provision of information. For instance, Article 26 of the OECD Model Tax Convention refers to a number of limitations on the obligation to provide information, including that contracting states are not obligated to carry out administrative means at variance with their laws and administrative practice, supply information not obtainable under their laws or in the normal course of administration, or supply information that would disclose trade or certain other secrets, or be contrary to public policy (ordre public).

112. See Commentary to Article 26, paragraph 9 of the OECD Model Tax Convention for details.

a) Trade, business and other secrets

42. As stated in the Commentary to Article 26 of the OECD Model Tax Convention, these secrets should not be interpreted in too wide a sense. Before invoking such rules a country should carefully weigh if the interests of the taxpayer really justify their application. Otherwise, it is clear that too wide an interpretation would in many cases impede effective exchange of information.

43. Furthermore, financial information, including books and records do not generally constitute a trade, business or other secret. However, in certain exceptional cases books and records may benefit from protection by secrecy rules. For instance a request for financial information could be denied if the response to the request would reveal a proprietary pricing model of a bank or other financial institution.

44. Rules on trade, business and other secrets have their main application where the provision of information in response to a request would reveal protected intellectual property created by the holder of the information or a third person. For instance, a bank might hold a pending patent application for safe keeping or a trade process might be described in a loan application. In these cases the requested State may decline any portion of a request for information that would reveal information protected by patent, copyright or other intellectual property laws.

b) Reciprocity

45. Very generally, the principle of reciprocity, in this context, provides that a requested State is not required to obtain and provide information that the applicant State would not be able to obtain under similar circumstances under its own laws for purposes of enforcing its own tax laws.

46. The principle of reciprocity is intended to prevent the applicant State from circumventing its domestic law limitations by seeking information from the other Contracting State, thus, making use of greater powers than it possesses under its own laws. For instance, most countries recognise under their domestic laws that information cannot be obtained from a person to the extent such person can claim the privilege against self-incrimination. A requested State may, therefore, refuse to exchange information if the applicant State would have been precluded by its own self-incrimination rules from obtaining the information under similar circumstances.

47. Furthermore, the principle of reciprocity is intended to balance the administrative burdens assumed by the Contracting States. It is recognised that replying to a request for information, especially in situations where the

information is not needed by the authorities of the State providing the information, might impose a burden on the resources of such state.

48. The principle of reciprocity has no application where the legal system or administrative practice of only one country provides for a specific procedure. For instance, a country requested to provide information could not point to the absence of a ruling regime in the country requesting information and decline to provide information on its ruling regime based on a reciprocity argument. Similarly, if one country does not have either a formal or an informal Advance Pricing Agreements ("APA") practice it is not precluded by the reciprocity requirement from seeking information on APA's entered into by the authorities of other countries. Of course, where the requested information itself is "not obtainable under the laws or in the normal course of the administration"[113] of the requesting State, a requested State may decline such a request.

c) Primary reliance on domestic sources of information

49. It is expected that the regular sources of information available under the internal taxation procedure should be relied upon before information is sought from another state. Thus, any country may decline a request for information -- without failing the effective exchange of information criterion -- if the state requesting the information has not pursued all means available in its own territory, provided such means would not give rise to disproportionate difficulties.

d) Attorney-client privilege

50. The attorney-client privilege generally attaches to information that constitutes a confidential communication between a client and an attorney, solicitor or other admitted legal representative. While the scope and the coverage of the privilege might differ among states, it should not be overly broad so as to hamper effective exchange of information. For a general description of the attorney-client privilege, see the Commentary to Article 7 of the Agreement on Exchange of Information on Tax Matters in the Appendix.

113. Article 26, paragraph 2, sub-paragraph b) OECD Model Tax Convention. See also the accompanying commentary at paragraph 15.

e) Public policy (ordre public)

51. The issue of public policy should rarely arise in connection with information requests. Generally, public policy can only be invoked in extreme cases in which the provision of information would contradict the vital interests of the State itself. For instance, a case of public policy would arise if a tax investigation in the State requesting information was motivated by political or racial persecution. Reasons of public policy might also be invoked where the information constitutes a state secret, for instance sensitive information held by secret services the disclosure of which would be contrary to the vital interests of the requested State.

52. Countries should use the guidance set out in the box below to assess whether a preferential regime that meets the no or low tax criterion lacks effective exchange of information.

> The following features are likely to result in a lack of effective exchange of information:
>
> - A country has no legal mechanism for exchange of information.
> - A country exchanges information only in connection with criminal tax matters.
> - The legal mechanism for exchange of information is rendered ineffective by overly broad secrecy, attorney-client privilege or public policy rules or practices.

iv) Protection of the confidentiality of the information provided

53. At the national level, tax administrations are required to provide a high degree of confidentiality to information received or gathered about a taxpayer for tax purposes. Without this assurance, it could be difficult for tax authorities to obtain the information needed to carry out the tax laws. This "tax secrecy" is of even greater importance in the international context and forms the basis of mutual trust between nations. Exchange of information is a highly sensitive issue for taxpayers and their governments, and their willingness to provide information could be adversely affected if it was thought that information provided might be used for purposes other than those for which it was exchanged. Given this legitimate concern, tax secrecy is an essential component of an exchange of information instrument. In order to ensure the confidentiality of a taxpayer's affairs, measures must be implemented at the national level to prevent protected information that has

been gathered for tax purposes from being disclosed to unauthorised persons or from being used for impermissible purposes. At the same time, adequate provision must be made to allow disclosure of the information to be made to persons, including courts and administrative bodies, involved in the administration and enforcement of the tax laws.

54. Where a country has no effective measures to protect the confidentiality of information received from another country, the latter country may refuse to exchange information. In such a case the refusal to exchange information concerning a preferential regime that meets the no or low tax factor does not indicate a failure to comply with the effective exchange of information criterion.

v) Administrative practices for effective exchange

55. In addition to establishing the legal mechanisms to allow a State to make and respond to a request for information, the states should have administrative procedures in place to ensure the smooth operation and handling of requests and responses. For example, procedures should exist for prompt review of incoming and outgoing requests to make sure that the request satisfies the terms of the convention and includes sufficient information for the request to be carried out. Thus, in the absence of unusual circumstances, a state requested to provide information should, within 60 days, notify the competent authority of the state requesting information of any deficiencies in a request. Similarly, and again in the absence of unusual circumstances, the competent authority of the requested state should notify the competent authority of the requesting state if it is unable to obtain and provide the requested information within 90 days from the receipt of the request. Such notification should include the reasons for the inability, the nature of the obstacles or the reasons for a refusal.

56. The laws in some countries require notification of the taxpayer affected by an information request before the information is provided to the country requesting the information. Such notification requirements are not inconsistent with effective exchange of information. However, the notification rules should be such that they do not frustrate the efforts of the country seeking the information. For instance, notification rules should permit exceptions from prior notification (*e.g.*, in cases in which the information request is of a very urgent nature or the notification is likely to undermine the chances of success of the investigation conducted by the country requesting the information).

57. Countries should use the guidance set out in the box below to assess whether a preferential regime that meets the no or low tax criterion

lacks effective exchange of information because of inadequate administrative procedures.

> The following feature is likely to result in a lack of effective exchange of information:
>
> A country has inadequate administrative procedures in place to ensure the prompt and efficient handling of, and responses to, requests for exchange of information.

D. Examples of regime-specific information

58. This Part provides examples of the types of information that countries should be able to obtain and provide with respect to the categories of preferential regimes identified in the 2000 Report.

Insurance regimes

- Premiums paid to the company and insurance benefits paid by the company.
- Contents of the contracts on the bases of which the premiums are paid, like the identity of the policyholders, the risks insured, and the duration of the contracts.
- Reserves, appropriations to the reserves, and the impact on the taxable income of appropriations to the reserves.

Financing and Leasing

- Loans granted by the company and interest received on these loans.
- Contents of the contracts on the bases of which the loans were granted, like the identity of the borrower, the reason for the loan and the duration of the contracts.
- Reserves, appropriations to the reserves, and the impact on the taxable income of appropriations to the reserves.
- The portfolio investments and other investments.
- Tangible and intangible assets provided to other companies.
- Holding activities.

Fund Managers

- Reserves, appropriations to the reserves, and the impact on the taxable income of appropriations to the reserves.
- The portfolio investments and other investments.
- The distribution of profits.
- Related party transactions, in particular information on services fees or

other fees paid to or received from related parties.

Banking

- Borrowing and lending activities and other financial activities.
- Deposits accepted from clients and the contents of the contracts on which these deposits were accepted, such as the identity of the client, interest due on the deposit and the duration of the contract.
- Reserves, appropriations to the reserves, and the impact on the taxable income of appropriations to the reserves.
- The portfolio investments and other investments.

Headquarters regimes

- Functions performed by the headquarters to the group (copies of relevant agreements).
- Operating expenses of the headquarters.
- The headquarters regime, conditions fulfilled, granted duration of the regime, etc.
- Cancellation of the headquarters regime if any and reasons for it.

Distribution Centres

- Detailed activities performed by the distribution centre.
- Copies of relevant agreements between the distribution centre and the group members.
- Prices invoiced to companies of the group in compensation of the activities performed.
- Operating expenses of the distribution centre.
- Risks borne by the distribution centre.
- Conditions fulfilled to obtain authorisation for a distribution centre regime, granted, duration, etc.
- Cancellation of the distribution centre regime, if any, and reasons for it.

Service Centres

- Nature of services provided by the service centre.
- Relevant agreements between the service centres and the group members.
- Risks borne by the service centre.
- Cancellation of the service centre regime if any and reasons for it.

Shipping Companies

- Flag of the ships.
- Contracts of haulage.
- Contracts of management including crew management, commercial management, where services are provided to a ship's owner by a management company.
- Registration documents including details of ship mortgages and any parallel registrations.
- Financial accounts, books and records, including information to identify intra-group transactions and to verify their compliance with the arm's length principle.

Holding Companies

- Organisational structure of group.
- Amount of dividends received and capital gains or losses realised.
- Distribution of income.

ORGANISATION FOR ECONOMIC CO-OPERATION AND DEVELOPMENT

The OECD is a unique forum where governments work together to address the economic, social and environmental challenges of globalisation. The OECD is also at the forefront of efforts to understand and to help governments respond to new developments and concerns, such as corporate governance, the information economy and the challenges of an ageing population. The Organisation provides a setting where governments can compare policy experiences, seek answers to common problems, identify good practice and work to co-ordinate domestic and international policies.

The OECD member countries are: Australia, Austria, Belgium, Canada, Chile, the Czech Republic, Denmark, Estonia, Finland, France, Germany, Greece, Hungary, Iceland, Ireland, Israel, Italy, Japan, Korea, Luxembourg, Mexico, the Netherlands, New Zealand, Norway, Poland, Portugal, the Slovak Republic, Slovenia, Spain, Sweden, Switzerland, Turkey, the United Kingdom and the United States. The European Union takes part in the work of the OECD.

OECD Publishing disseminates widely the results of the Organisation's statistics gathering and research on economic, social and environmental issues, as well as the conventions, guidelines and standards agreed by its members.

OECD PUBLISHING, 2, rue André-Pascal, 75775 PARIS CEDEX 16
(23 2011 15 1 P) ISBN 978-92-64-10723-6 – No. 58163 2011-05

